THE LAW OF LOVE

Steve Young

DESERET
BOOK

SALT LAKE CITY, UTAH

DESERET BOOK is a registered trademark of Deseret Book Company.

Visit us at deseretbook.com

Library of Congress Cataloging-in-Publication Data
(CIP on file)
ISBN: 978-1-63993-031-9 (paperback)

Printed in the United States of America
Brigham Young University Press, Provo, UT

10   9   8   7   6   5   4   3   2   1

To Barb, Braedon, Jackson, Summer, and Laila

I wrote this for you and because of you.
You teach me how to love every day.

The law of love is loving as God loves, seeking another's healing, expecting nothing in return.

"We live in a world that is held together by love—organized by love, maintained by love, and nurtured by love. Ultimately it will be redeemed by love and even now it is in the process of being redeemed by the love and kindness that we offer each other."

—Chieko N. Okazaki (1926–2011),
counselor in the Relief Society General Presidency,
Being Enough (Salt Lake City: Bookcraft, 2002)

"Love is the greatest of all the commandments—all others hang upon it. It is our focus as followers of the living Christ."

—Joseph B. Wirthlin (1917–2008),
of the Quorum of the Twelve Apostles,
"The Great Commandment,"
Ensign, November 2007

Contents

CONTENTS

1

FROM TOUGH TEAMMATE
TO CEASE-FIRE

When I joined the team in 1987, the San Francisco 49ers had already won two Super Bowls and were on their way to two more. My new teammates included some of the most famous athletes in the world at the time—names like Joe Montana and Jerry Rice—as well as other future Hall of Famers and Pro Bowl players at almost every position.

Head coach Bill Walsh thrust me into this very visible and sophisticated locker room. He recruited me by telling me that quarterback Joe Montana had had two back surgeries and wouldn't be able to play much longer. I was sorry to hear about Joe's injuries but also enthusiastic about joining the best team that any quarterback could ever want.

From the very first day I could tell that I was in for a wild ride, especially jumping in as the new guy ready to replace the king. Fellow players and fans alike naturally felt they needed to let me know where their allegiance lay. I just wanted to survive. I felt the heat from whispers in every corner. But in one place it wasn't a whisper; it was like the roar of a lion.

Defensive player Charles Haley was one of the many future Hall of Famers on the team. If Charles spotted a weakness, he would exploit it with torrid attacks in the training or locker room. Bystanders awkwardly laughed, but to the victim it was brutal. Most would respond in kind, trying to throw it back with more velocity. But that just emboldened Charles to ramp up the attack.

The target that Charles attacked most vociferously was me, even though we had been teammates for five years. To him I was a threat to Joe, who needed to be defended. Anytime he got a chance, Charles sliced me down to size in front of whoever was around.

As the new guy on the team I didn't want to counterattack; besides, that just wasn't my style. It got so bad that I tried to avoid Charles as much as possible. Every day I pulled into the parking lot and looked for his car. If it was there, I checked with friendly trainers or equipment guys to see where he was so I could avoid him. Most of the time Charles set up camp in the training room, where we went for physical therapy, ice, tape for our ankles, and so on. If I needed treatment for bumps and bruises, I would handle it myself somewhere else. Better to just stay off Charles's radar.

Even though I was recruited to replace Joe Montana, he recovered after his two back surgeries and returned to play, much to everyone's surprise. This left me in the wings for four frustrating years. Finally Joe stepped down, and I took over as quarterback in 1991.

Tensions escalated. After Joe's departure, we were struggling as a team, and I was struggling even more. Replacing Joe was no joke.

It all reached a boiling point in front of 90,000 people in the Los Angeles Coliseum[1] as we lost to the LA Raiders 12–6. Just as the clock ran out, Jerry Rice was open in the end zone, but I didn't see him. In desperation, I threw the ball weakly to no one.

After the game Charles was furious and distraught, ranting about Steve Young being terrible and why it was all so awful. He was on a tirade and just wouldn't quit.

Finally after no relenting, Ronnie Lott was called over from the Raiders' locker room. Ronnie had been traded earlier that year from the 49ers to the Raiders and was trusted by all of us. He was able to calm the waters.

After that game, the weight of it all was as heavy as I can ever remember. I was no stranger to losing games, but this was different. I was dropped off at the house late at night. I slumped down in the driveway and sat next to the parked car. I leaned back against the tire, just forlorn. I didn't know what to do, what my next move was. I thought, *well, let me just go to sleep. Just try to get ready for what is coming tomorrow. Maybe tomorrow will be a better day.*

Obviously, things became more complicated in our locker room and especially for me.

A few weeks later, we landed in Seattle to play the Seahawks and everyone jumped on the buses from the airport to the hotel. I had been distracted and was last to jump on. There was one seat left . . . next to Charles. He looked at me and motioned to the empty seat. There was no other choice, but all the same, I was surprised at the

---

1 During later remodeling, the LA Coliseum capacity was reduced significantly.

invitation and steeled myself for more verbal jabs. I sat down in silence. I thought I was going to get an earful for the twenty-minute bus ride in the dark. But Charles didn't say anything.

I had heard that his wife was ailing, so I said, "I'm sorry to hear about your wife. I hope she is doing better."

He replied, "Thanks. It's been tough." Silence. Then he told me how they had been together in college and she had been struggling for some time. I asked him about his college days. I enjoyed hearing his story. Then he asked me if I had a family and was surprised to learn that I was single. I realized that neither of us knew much about each other, even though we had been on the same team for five years.

We chatted the whole way to the hotel, and something miraculous happened. It was as if we had seen each other—really seen each other—for the first time. There wasn't the mutual demonization that can happen in a vacuum. I wasn't asking Charles about his wife to impress him or win him over; I genuinely wanted to know how he and his family were doing.

Nothing memorable was said. What was memorable was the change in our relationship. What had been a war was now more peaceful. Sure, he kept teasing me, but in a less caustic, damaging way. I even started to give it back to him, playfully in careful doses. But the war was over. It had escalated way beyond where it should have. My professional life already felt difficult beyond difficult, and to have a sense of peace in my relationship with a former enemy was just miraculous. That miracle happened because of a brief conversation between two humans who were forced to sit next to each other.

We are now great friends and laugh about those dark days. For me it felt like life and death. Finding some measure of peace was oxygen-producing.

Without knowing exactly what it was, I had implemented the law of love, which is loving as God loves, seeking another's healing, expecting nothing in return. Instead of either of us jabbing at the other, consistent with the troubled relationship between us up to that moment, we were able to intentionally connect as human beings and share from our hearts in a vulnerable way.

That enduring lesson is what this book is about. That brief experience and many more complicated situations led me to think more about the law of love. I have studied it, thought about it, and tried to implement it for many years. This book is the result.

The law of love is undefeated in human relations throughout history. The law of love can provide a path forward when everything else has been exhausted.

2

WHY THIS BOOK?

This book has been burning a hole in my mind for quite a while. Over my lifetime, in so many different contexts, I've noticed that complex issues were solved with simple understandings of the same gospel principle. This principle worked in all of the spheres of my life—in my football career, my business career, my spiritual life and relationships at church, and my family. I found myself thinking about this principle again and again. No matter what the question was, my answer was always the same: the law of love. The more I worked with the law of love, learning about it and trying to live it, the more I could see that it worked. As I talked about it with others, they told me the law of love really resonated with them, whether they were religious, atheist, humanist, or anything else. I finally decided to get this idea out of my head and onto paper so I could sleep better at night.

The law of love is loving as God loves, seeking another's

healing, expecting nothing in return.[1] This is not new doctrine. But for me, looking at everything through the lens of the law of love was a subtle shift with vast implications. Some of these concepts were hidden in plain sight, right there in the scriptures. Now that I see them, my whole world is changed for the better.

The law of love is different from love itself. How many songs try to define the word *love*? It can be compassionate, charitable, romantic, sexual—love is a feeling, selfish or unselfish. But the *law* of love is a governing force. Just like the laws of gravity, physics, and thermodynamics govern this world, the law of love governs all of creation—the heavens and the earth. The law of love is the highest of all the laws. When I seek to live the law of love—when I make it my quest to steer my life by this highest governing power—the law of love can transform everything.

Many people that I know, inside and outside the Church, intuitively live this law of love. Regardless of whether they are coming from a place of doubt or belief, I can see the fruits of this law in their lives, whether they recognize it or not. I can especially see the effect of the law of love on the lives of those around them. I draw inspiration from many people you'll find quoted in this book, including some who are members of The Church of Jesus Christ of Latter-day Saints, Anglican, atheist, Baptist, Catholic, Confucian, Hindu, Jewish, Muslim, and secular people of wisdom. Truth is truth, wherever I find it. Joseph Smith said, "One of the grand fundamental principles of Mormonism is to receive truth, let it come

---

1 See page 187 for thoughts about how to implement the law of love.

from whence it may" ("History, 1838–1856, volume E-1 [1 July 1843–30 April 1844]," p. 1666, *The Joseph Smith Papers*).

You may feel like you're already overwhelmed, already underwater, and you don't need to read one more book that will add one more thing to your task list. But what if understanding the law of love unlocked everything, unleashing a healing power that made everything on your list easier? You may feel like Moses at the edge of the Red Sea: you've got water in front of you, the Egyptians behind you in hot pursuit, and you're stuck. But what if the law of love could open a path for you? Maybe you could "make a way out of no way," as the African-American saying goes. There is power in the law of love. Give this idea a chance to change your life, because it has changed mine.

So often I might have tripped on various looming obstacles that I found in my path, sometimes boulder-sized stumbling blocks that came from different directions. I didn't come across the law of love from a pleasant walk in the park. I dug deep into the law of love out of desperation, trying to find a way forward during some dark times. Focusing on the law of love helped me zero in on what really matters: the perpetual, unchanging principles of love at the core of Jesus's gospel.

At times I look back over my life and think, what is my legacy? What have I accomplished? I've got trophies and rings and all, but what have I done with my life? And I think to myself, the full measure of my life (or anyone's life) is to have a healing intent, seeking to heal others. That's what I pray for every night—to reach the full measure of who I can be. If I have selflessly sought to heal someone,

I have done the work that God sent me here to do. I've found such great peace in that knowledge for myself. Beyond that, anything else that I have accomplished is extra. The foundational principle of the restored gospel is that we are here to learn and grow. My life purpose is to figure out how best to allow that to happen. The legacy of my life is seeking to heal others.

Trust me—I am not an expert on the law of love. I am in process. All I'm doing is trying to describe it, knowing that's where I need to go. I just have been blessed to see the direction. But like you, I'm just another traveler on the journey to that place.

WHERE AM I COMING FROM?

When I was in ninth grade, I wanted to be a three-sport varsity player: football, basketball, and baseball. I knew that to reach my goal, I needed to work extra hard. One of the ways I tested myself was to run laps around my neighborhood in Greenwich, Connecticut. One lap was about three-fourths of a mile to the elementary school, up Palmer Hill, and back down to my house. Palmer Hill should have been named Palmer Mountain. It felt like it went straight up in the air.

When I was young, I decided that each time before I ran, I had to commit to myself how many laps I would run. Most of the time it was three or four laps. But sometimes I would tell myself five or six. Once I said that to myself, it was now in blood. I had to do it. I never quit, not once. I may have had to walk at times, but I never quit. I felt like if I did quit, it would cause some kind of existential domino to fall and knock over who knows how many more, to the detriment of my goal to get to varsity in all three sports, which in the end I did achieve.

Being goal-oriented has been a great way for me to live. I've kept up the spirit of that run up Palmer Hill my whole life. I've always been a can-do guy. If you told me what I needed to do to be successful at something, that was all I needed. I would start climbing.

In many ways, that also describes my spiritual life. As a young kid I was the only member of The Church of Jesus Christ of Latter-day Saints in my high school of 3,000. I loved listening to *Saturday's Warrior*[2] as I did my homework. The music and the story really resonated with me. I wanted to be a Saturday warrior: someone God could count on to do good in these last days. I knew the sacrifices that warriors made: living the Word of Wisdom (no coffee, tea, alcohol, smoking, or drugs), upholding chastity and dating standards, using clean language and entertainment, etc. Certainly I appreciated the sense of connection with God that grew in my heart as a result of my faithfulness to those standards. To this day it's a connection I cherish. The hope of eternal life, or celestial living, or Zion, is the ultimate destination that I seek. How I get there begins with a well-lit path of covenant and sacrifice. Each of these things are vital and important to me.

But I also noticed that seeking for these rewards could become very self-consuming. In a way, it could become a contractual agreement between me and God. If I do these important things and keep doing them, I can receive glorious rewards that are worth any

---

2 *Saturday's Warrior*, a musical by Douglass Stewart and Lex de Azevedo, 1973.

sacrifice. But at some point, I felt that seeking eternal life became an end in itself—to earn the rewards for myself.

In the end, we cannot get where we want to be by pursuing a transactional relationship with God. Even if I'm as obedient as I can be, I am still an "unprofitable servant" (Mosiah 2:21). I need a Savior to make up the difference between my best efforts and what God requires. Besides, if I'm only pursuing the rewards, I'm not necessarily becoming more Christlike, more loving.

In fact, the opposite may be true. For example, we may see others as problems to be fixed (preferably in OUR way) instead of people to be loved.[3] We may see other people as obstacles to our journey instead of relationships of love and support. A wayward family member who torpedoes our goal of "no empty chairs" in our family circle in heaven. A challenging youth who shows up late and unprepared to class, every single time. Someone whose path is calling them in a different direction from mine—still a wonderful path, and right for them, just different from mine. An unruly child in Primary who simply can't sit still and keep their hands to themselves for thirty-five seconds at a stretch. The irritating coworker with yet another trivial interruption. The slow driver in front of us when we're in a hurry. All these folks aren't trying to be obstacles in our journey; they're trying to figure out their own lives. These situations call for support and love from us, not disappointment or annoyance at being inconvenienced.

Even if we understand the idea that we should love people, we

---

3 President Thomas S. Monson spoke about this in his talk "Finding Joy in the Journey" (*Ensign*, Nov. 2008).

sometimes think we're supposed to love them back onto our path instead of respecting their own journey. I'm not trying to love people into coming with me. I'm just loving people. No expectations, no transaction. They and God will figure out their journey; my job is to love them along the way.

At church, some might wish a certain family would just move away so they could be a Zion congregation, instead of seeing that family as wounded travelers on the way to Jericho (see Luke 10:29–37) whom we have been called to help. That's what I'm talking about. We literally can't be a Zion congregation without ALL of us, together. In seeking to heal others in their challenges, I grow in valuable ways and learn things that I can't learn any other way. If the goal of mortality is to become more like God, then we need to study how God lives in nontransactional relationships (more on this later).

The Church is like a hospital. Sometimes you're the doctor and sometimes you're the patient. No need to get judgmental or holier-than-thou when it's your turn to be the doctor. Soon enough you'll need help too.

In the end, transactional relationships are self-focused and inadvertently become a source of othering. Our accomplishments make us feel that we are elite, elect, special. Every human wants to be special. We want to earn status with God. But it doesn't work that way. A famous quote from a modern-day Apostle makes that clear: "Salvation cannot be bought with the currency of obedience; it is purchased by the blood of the Son of God" (Elder Dieter F. Uchtdorf, "The Gift of Grace," *Ensign*, May 2015).

3

SCIENCE AND
THE LAW OF LOVE

Learning about and seeking to live the law of love has opened me up to seeing it everywhere I look. I find this truth everywhere. So did Brigham Young: "I want to say to my friends that we believe in all good. If you can find a truth in heaven, earth or hell, it belongs to our doctrine. We believe it; it is ours; we claim it. [The gospel] embraces all morality, all virtue, all light, all intelligence, all greatness, and all goodness. . . . It is our duty and calling . . . to gather up all the truths in the world pertaining to . . . the sciences, and to philosophy, wherever it may be found . . . and bring it to Zion" (*Discourses of Brigham Young*, selected by John A. Widtsoe [1941], 2, 3, 248).

Spirituality needs to be practical, in the dirt. My spirituality is based in science. God is the great Scientist, as the Creator of the universe and everything in it using scientific principles. Some of those principles we understand and many we don't yet. Science is not a fixed body of knowledge but is continuously evolving.

A fascinating book I have enjoyed is *The Language of God: A Scientist Presents Evidence for Belief*, by Francis S. Collins, the scientist who headed up the Human Genome Project. While I may not agree with all his professional views, I respect his journey from disbelief to faith. He was an atheist and claimed it was because of science. But in his work on the DNA sequence, Collins said to himself, this is a place of beauty, a piece of art. This DNA sequence is not a place of randomness. This is intentional, but nothing in evolution says there is intent. The deeper he looked into science, the more beauty he saw and the more intent.

Another thing he noticed was that there is no scientific reason for love. Collins wrote:

> My assertion of "I don't know" was really more along the lines of "I don't want to know." My conclusion [was] that no thinking scientist could seriously entertain the possibility of God without committing some sort of intellectual suicide. So I gradually shifted from agnosticism to atheism, discounting [spiritual beliefs] as sentimentality and outmoded superstition.
>
> [But] did I not consider myself a scientist? Does a scientist draw conclusions without considering the data? Could there be a more important question in all of human existence than "Is there a God?" I determined to have a look at the facts, no matter what the outcome. I had started this journey of intellectual exploration to confirm my atheism. That now lay in ruins as . . . many

issues forced me to admit the plausibility of the God hypothesis. Faith in God now seemed more rational than disbelief.

The elegance behind life's complexity is indeed reason for awe, and for belief in God. I was astounded by the elegance of the human DNA code. For me, the experience of sequencing the human genome . . . was both a stunning scientific achievement and an occasion of worship. (Francis S. Collins, *The Language of God: A Scientist Presents Evidence for Belief* [New York: Free Press/Simon & Schuster, 2006], 16, 20, 21, 30, 86, 19, 3)

Collins was changed. His journey led him to faith and to God *because of* (not in spite of) science.

From the NASA photos of the immensity and enormousness of space down to microscopic DNA, I see the beauty of how science is put together at its most fundamental levels. Science is full of wonder beyond our capacity to grasp, from the vastness of the universe to the nanoscience of the subcellular level. I think that science itself is simultaneously getting bigger AND smaller. Bigger because of technology and the work that we've done to understand our world, adding to the body of scientific knowledge. But simultaneously science is getting smaller as it becomes clearer that science can't answer many things about the world. Everything about science is too perfect and too wonderful to be explained by mere chance. Science is continually getting bigger and smaller. In those two extremes, God is revealed to us, even through science.

THERMODYNAMICS: ENTROPY (THIS WORLD)
AND CENTROPY (THE WORLD WE SEEK)

We live in an entropic world. This world exists according to entropy, which is the second law of thermodynamics. Entropy means that our bodies and everything in our existence rots, decays, rusts, goes to disorganization. We drop a glass and it breaks and doesn't come back together. Everything ages. Everything ends.

The opposite condition is called centropy,[1] in which nothing ends or corrodes. It's a perpetual place, an eternal place. It's science. It's that place where God and eternal things last forever. And that's what we seek. That's the miracle of the Resurrection and all the promises of Christ and His Atonement and healing: that we can be in that place, a centropic place. When I think about Zion, about that celestial space, I realize it has to be full of people who are living the law of love: seeking others' healing without transaction, without any sense of value exchanged: where we receive solely, wholly, fully. We give the same way: solely, wholly, fully.

Latter-day Saint scientist Markus Covert told me that science was able to prove that "chance does not exclude inevitability," according to Christian de Duve, cowinner of the 1974 Nobel Prize for Physiology or Medicine ("The Constraints of Chance," *Scientific American* [Jan. 1996], 112). That is, although the world is random and chaotic, there can also be an inevitable place of order. Both can exist simultaneously. For my friend Markus, that had a big impact. Even though he believes in agency and opposition, and he sees the

---

1 Also spelled syntropy (like synergy) or negentropy.

chaos and pain in the world, science has proven that randomness, chaos, and pain don't preclude some celestial place of perpetuity.

I started to talk about this principle in a scientific way with an atheist friend. I asked him, "What if there is a place of perpetuity?" In this life we know disorder and entropy, but what if there were a place of centropy to which our spirits return? We are of God, with something infinite inside of us. Part of our DNA is this eternal place. It's meant to be centropic, perpetual. And even my atheist friend could see it, thinking, *wouldn't that be great?*

I thought to myself, *yes, it is great, because that's heaven to me.* Seeking another's healing, goodness, growth, and grace is a quest that is perpetual and won't rot to self-righteousness. It won't decay over time or devolve; it won't seek itself in a selfish way (see Moroni 7:45).

Thinking about earthly entropy/celestial centropy brings science and God closer, not further apart. The more we know, the more we come into a oneness with the great Scientist.

4

COMPLEMENTARY TRACKS:
THE PREPARATORY TRACK
AND THE FINISHING TRACK

There are two complementary tracks in life that relate to my quest for my ultimate goal of returning to live with God—one transactional/preparatory, and another nontransactional/ finishing. Both tracks work together. **God paved both tracks**, because God knows humans. The transactional track prepares me through obedience and a can-do spirit. The transactional track draws me into a relationship with God. The Church does a wonderful job of preparing its members on this vital track, and this track is especially important for kids to learn how to be faithful. In high school, my goal-oriented approach to life was very rewarding but also very self-consuming, always seeking the next achievement. Even keeping the commandments sometimes felt like I was seeking the blessing: treating God like an ATM that dispensed blessings if I inserted the "currency of obedience" instead of enjoying that heavenly relationship because of my love for God.

In the end, a transactional track alone creates an inevitable self-absorption. That is why a complementary track is needed. The nontransactional/finishing track is the most vital, with boundaries that are celestial, perpetual, and eternal. It can only be traveled in selflessness, focusing on others. Nontransactional choices are not reward-based. Think about it as a direction you face each day. I rise to the direction of others. To whom can I bring healing and hope today, no matter what journey they are on? The key to traveling this finishing track is intent. It has to be focused on others. Lose yourself and you find yourself (see Matthew 10:39 and 16:25).

The first track—the transactional track—is an important place to start. Some relationships ARE transactional in this life, and that's fine. I go to work, I get paid. I hire someone to cut my hair, I pay that person. That's the way our economy works. It's only a problem when I take that transactional thinking too far and commodify every relationship, treating people like ATMs: insert the things they want, take out the things I want. That amounts to treating another person like an object, not a human being. That's transactional thinking taken too far. In the end it's impossible to keep a transactional relationship from rotting in self-interest. And that goes for even the deepest relationships, including our relationship with God.

This finishing track of selflessness is the law of love. On this track, we can join Christ in healing the world and heal ourselves as a by-product. This track is the track of abundance, of perpetuity, of healing and love. Zion must be on this track because Zion is a place of perpetuity. The celestial kingdom must be on this track because it also is a place of perpetuity. By definition, neither place is on the preparatory or transactional track.

As I began to understand this—when I tried to quit looking for the transaction—I could see others more deeply. The great irony of heaven is that in the selfless effort to serve and heal, the goal that I always had for my own healing is now available. The destination isn't far off; it is right here, in people around me to love. It's seeing—truly seeing—the person next to me and seeking their healing, thereby finding that place where I can do that forever.

Once I saw these two complementary tracks, I noticed where scripture and the words of the prophets relate to either the transactional track or the finishing track or both. God draws us in on the transactional track because it's foundational, preparatory. Whenever we are ready, God pulls us toward the finishing track to attain the full measure of our creation—not just to grow and improve incrementally by staying on the preparatory/transactional track, but breaking through to a brighter new reality. The law of love is a superior extension or higher level of the law of obedience, not in opposition to it. It draws obedience and all laws to it with a gravitational pull as a loving invitation, leading us to the next step on the finishing track.

WHAT WAS IN THE FIRST SET OF TABLETS? MOSES AND THE PREPARATORY AND FINISHING PATHS

Remember when Moses spent forty days communing with God on Mount Sinai (see Exodus 24:18)? During that time, Moses received "two tables of . . . stone, written with the finger of God" (Exodus 31:18). Meanwhile, down the mountain, the children of Israel and Aaron were engaging in idol worship with a homemade golden calf. "Moses' anger waxed hot, and he cast the tables out of his hands, and brake them beneath the mount" (Exodus 32:19). Moses made a second set of stone tablets and spent another forty days on Mount Sinai (see Exodus 34). God said, "I will write upon them also, the words of the law, . . . but it shall not be according to the first. . . but it shall be after the law of a carnal commandment" (Joseph Smith Translation, Exodus 34:1–2).[1]

God had to write down the Ten Commandments in the second set of stone tablets because the children of Israel were not ready to live the higher law. But it was never meant to stay that way. The "carnal commandments" were God's temporary plan. That's the lower law, the preparatory path. If the children of Israel had been ready to live the higher law of love on the finishing path, God wouldn't have had to tell them not to kill people. They already would have known not to kill people. God wouldn't have had to tell them not to steal. They already would have known not to steal or covet or cheat on their spouses.

I think the first set of tablets contained God's Plan A for His children: the higher law of love, which would include an invitation to all the qualities of heaven that we need to practice here on earth. Those behaviors would feel natural, without compulsion, not by command but as a natural attraction.

---

1 Also missing from the second set of stone tables were the higher priesthood and "the ordinances thereof" (Joseph Smith Translation, Exodus 34:1). I would argue that the higher priesthood and the ordinances thereof ARE the law of love. Keep reading to see how the law of love connects to priesthood principles of gentleness, meekness, love unfeigned, and using the priesthood to bless others, not yourself.

THE BOXCARS OF OBEDIENCE AND THE ENGINE OF THE LAW OF LOVE

Think of a train—let's call it the train to eternity. The boxcars are all the laws and commandments. Those things are good and an essential part of the train. But they're not the engine that drives the whole train. The engine is the law of love. It doesn't replace the obedience boxcars; it just pulls them forward in a different way.

The boxcars of obedience have no ability to perpetually take you forward. Without the engine of the law of love, the boxcars of obedience run out of steam. The engine has perpetual fuel, perpetual energy that can pull forward everything behind it.

Don't worry—all your expressions of faith in keeping any commandment are worthy. Those acts are a sacred trust. Nothing is lost. You only gain an exponentially more transformative relationship with God and others as you remain obedient out of love, with no expectation of reward.

Whenever I come across a scripture or a talk, I think about whether it belongs in the boxcars of obedience or the engine of the law of love. The boxcars are valuable, but they certainly are not going to take me the distance without being pulled by nontransactional, selfless love. Only the perpetual engine of the law of love can do that. The law of love stands supreme.

This engine analogy suggests that the law of love *pulls* all the other commandments. In a similar analogy, modern Apostle Elder Joseph B. Wirthlin said it *holds up* all the other commandments. He said, "Love is the greatest of all the commandments—all others hang upon it. It is our focus as followers of the living Christ" ("The Great Commandment," *Ensign*, Nov. 2007).

In the Sermon on the Mount, Christ said, "Think not that I am come to destroy the law, or the prophets: I am not come to destroy, but to fulfil" (Matthew 5:17). In the same way, the law of love doesn't destroy the law of obedience but fulfills it. The law of love pulls obedience forward in a different way. As mentioned earlier, I think about this quote from Elder Uchtdorf again and again: "Salvation cannot be bought with the currency of obedience" ("The Gift of Grace," *Ensign*, May 2015).

All the obedience in the world won't do me a bit of good without charity, that pure love we've been talking about: "Though I speak with the tongues of men and of angels, . . . though I have the gift of prophecy, and understand all mysteries, and all knowledge; and though I have all faith, so that I could remove mountains, and have not charity, I am nothing. And though I bestow all my goods to feed the poor, . . . and have not charity, it profiteth me nothing" (1 Corinthians 13:1–3). That's a long list of good works: the gift of tongues, prophecy, knowledge, faith, even giving away everything you have to the poor—but all of it amounts to nothing without love, said Paul. You leave all those good works in the boxcars of obedience if you don't have the engine of the law of love.

President Ezra Taft Benson explained it this way:

> The breadth, depth, and height of this love of God extend into every facet of one's life.
>
> Why did God put the first commandment [to love God] first? **Because He knew that if we truly loved Him**

we would *want* to keep all of His other command-ments." ("The Great Commandment—Love the Lord," *Ensign*, May 1988; emphasis added)

The engine of the law of love draws all the other commandments forward with a gravitational pull. This supreme law extends an invitation to live into the full measure of obedience—not out of fear of punishment, nor hoping to get credit, but out of pure love.

As we develop a proximate, intimate, wonderful relationship with our Savior, we are better prepared to do His work by extending His Atonement to others and seeking to heal. We can become like Christ on the finishing track as we press forward toward the celestial kingdom, to Zion, all of us together. Both tracks have their place on our journey back to the presence of God.

INVITING US HIGHER

That train analogy, with its boxcars of obedience and engine of the law of love, has helped me express what I mean here—but like all analogies, it only goes so far. A train is an inanimate object. It chugs along or it just sits there.

What's missing is the inviting, ennobling gravitational pull that the law of love extends. It gathers all goodness and truth to it.

By contrast, the law of obedience says *obey or else*, with a hammer or a threat, or even a deal: if you do obey, you'll get the blessings. That transactional feeling toward God as we obey just doesn't resonate. It's not that we want to be disobedient; we sometimes just don't appreciate the *hammer* of obedience, when obedience is presented to us in that way. I think people are naturally demand-resistant.

Sometimes we're almost disobedient just because we don't like being told what to do. Or we may analyze the cost/benefit of the transaction and weigh whether obedience is worth the effort.

But the law of love is a pure invitation from God for something wonderful that could come into your life. When the law of love is unencumbered and pure, it draws you in as an invitation to love and appreciate all the laws. You live obedience differently when it is pulled forward by the law of love. It is so beautiful because it elevates and ennobles all the laws, coming from a different direction. That's when transactional thinkers say, "Oh my gosh, this is not just another way to live the gospel; this is the *only* way to actually elevate everything all at once, in every direction." Pride and self-interested expectations of reward or fear of punishment are corrosive in every direction, but the law of love is beautiful, perpetual, life-giving, renewing, and elevating, in every direction.

"A HIGHER AND HOLIER WAY," CALLING US FROM THE PREPARATORY TO THE FINISHING TRACK

Just recently we've seen a milestone in the Church worldwide. In recent years, the Church has been making a shift from the transactional track to the nontransactional track. (Remember, God paved both tracks—both tracks have their place.) This milestone was the change from home/visiting teaching to ministering. I'll talk more about that in detail later (see page 121). But notice that there was nothing wrong with home and visiting teaching. Before that shift, we had been doing what we thought was right our whole lives. It WAS right. It was good. We were doing what we had been asked to do. But the Lord knew that we were ready to be called to a higher, holier work. When it was introduced, it was called the law of love (see Jeffrey R. Holland, "Be With and Strengthen Them," *Ensign*, May 2018).

What is the difference? Home/visiting teaching was for credit, with an end-of-the-month report to a district supervisor. That's an honorable effort of faith. But it's transactional: I visit my families, I submit my report, I get the pat on the back from my district supervisor for having "done" my visits. Now ministering is no longer for credit. It's no longer a transaction. The emphasis is now on loving and healing the family, not making a visit and reporting it. That change is a clear indication that complementary tracks exist, because now we're on a higher, holier track, while formerly we were doing the lower, less holy work (yet still a faithful offering).

Although it appears subtle, this is not a little change; this is one of the more profound changes in the Church in decades, because of its effect on us. Now ministering is not a transactional work. It's purely the law of love: loving as God loves, with the intent to heal, seeking nothing in return.

Over time, loving as God loves becomes less a choice and more just who we are. We love because we ARE love, just as "God *is* love" (1 John 4:16; emphasis added). As we choose again and again to live the law of love, it causes us to fundamentally change WHO we are (becoming, "in Christ, . . . a new creature," as 2 Corinthians 5:17 says) so that loving the way that God loves is simply part of our being.

Put another way, the preparatory track draws me into an intimate, frictionless relationship with God. I'm not just obedient so I can go to heaven. I make and keep my covenants as an expression of my love for God. Then I'm in a better position to lift the burdens of others by accessing the flow-through power of Christ and His Atonement. I reach *up* to heaven in my relationship with God by covenant-keeping, not as an end place, but so that I am better prepared to reach *out* in relationship with my fellow humans. Otherwise I get everything ready (on the preparatory track) and never take the journey (on the finishing track).

JOINING WITH GOD IN THE HOLY WORK OF HEALING OTHERS

Embedded in those very covenants with God are opportunities to heal others. The baptismal covenant calls me to "bear one another's burdens, . . . mourn with those that mourn, yea, and comfort those that stand in need of comfort" (Mosiah 18:8–9). Bear, mourn, and comfort. That intimate covenant I made with God at my baptism draws me toward healing others. If I see baptism as a box to check ("yup, ordinance complete"), I missed the whole point. It's like God is saying, "Help Me do this wonderful work of healing through selfless love for others, because I've been doing it for millennia, for eons of time. And it's great stuff, so why don't you start doing it? Join Me in doing this healing work."

We don't heal—it's Christ who heals. And God calls us in the scriptures to join in this healing work:

- "He gave [the apostles] power . . . to heal all manner of sickness" (Matthew 10:1).
- "Heal the sick, cleanse the lepers" (Matthew 10:8).

- "[Peter] took [the lame man] by the right hand, and lifted him up" (Acts 3:7).
- "Bringing sick [to Peter] . . . they were healed" (Acts 5:16).
- "To another the gifts of healing" (1 Corinthians 12:9).
- "Gave unto Moses power that he should heal the nations" (2 Nephi 25:20).
- "To others it is given to have faith to heal" (D&C 46:20).
- "In my name they shall heal the sick" (D&C 84:68).
- "He [William Law] shall heal the sick, he shall cast out devils" (D&C 124:98).
- "We believe in the gift of . . . healing" (Articles of Faith 1:7).

Latter-day Saint authors Fiona and Terryl Givens said it this way:

> **[In] the healing and unifying of the entire human family . . . we are invited to be coparticipants with the Godhead. . . .** When we participate in the ordinance of adoption into the Heavenly Family—otherwise known as baptism, . . . we commit to join in the enterprise of Zion-building, to erect, edify, and constitute a community of love—of at-one-ment. Mosiah's language [the baptismal covenant in Mosiah 18:8–9] beautifully reminds us that we have been called to **work collaboratively *with* the Godhead in Their healing enterprise.** ("Atonement: From Penal Substitution to Radical Healing—An Excerpt from *All Things New* by Terryl and Fiona Givens," faithmatters.org; emphasis added)

In some faiths, you just accept Christ and the journey is over.

You made it. In our Church, sometimes we think all we have to do is accept Christ, receive the ordinances, and *then* the journey is over. We made it. The rest of the journey is just holding on and enduring to the end. We think it's the end of the road, the arrival, but it's actually the departure place. It's the place to join Christ in His work to heal the world.

By staying stuck on the preparatory track, we miss the finishing road to the place of perpetuity and peace, the Zion community that we seek.

"OTHERING" VS. ABUNDANT THINKING

When we think that checking off ordinances is the way to arrive at a special status, elite and complete, we are damning ourselves from the beauty of the law of love.

It's like we're looking for a few good people on one more pass through earth, and then we'll get on a spaceship to Kolob[2] and we're off on our own, we're good. But before blastoff, we're sifting the wheat from the chaff one more time here in the last days. We see others and we say, "Hey, good luck, thumbs-up. Hope you get to go too. Oh, and can I give you a lesson real quick? I'm on my way. I've got to go to heaven. I've checked all my boxes, I'm done. Good luck to you."

I don't think that's what God wants. I'm damning myself from this beauty and wonder of the fullness of the gospel by being stuck on the preparatory track, staying put because I think I'm all set. Then I find myself "othering" everyone else because I'm special.

---

2 A name for God's dwelling place—see Abraham 3:2–9.

This thinking might come from a perception of a scarcity of exaltation. But Jesus miraculously fed 5,000 with just a few loaves and fishes (see Matthew 14:13–21). Then, in the next chapter, He fed 4,000 more (see Matthew 15:32–39). He is telling us that there is room for everyone. There is no limit on salvation or exaltation. We want to help everyone get there. It's not, "I'll just take care of my salvation; you take care of yours." Taking care of my salvation IS reaching out and helping others find their salvation as well. And that partly saves me. That's my covenant—not just to reach heaven on my own, in isolation, but to actually reach out and help and heal others.

Podcaster and author Richard Ostler has said, "Heaven isn't about separating us from others and the feeling of satisfaction as we see those who didn't make it. Heaven is about reaching out and bringing others with us" (@Papa_Ostler, Twitter, Oct. 10, 2019). All those relationships have got to be nontransactional.

As a parent with my own children, I see this with new eyes of understanding. I care just as much about how my kids treat each other as I do about their relationship with me. I support them in learning how to love, and I relish seeing them extend that same caring to each other, which will hopefully outlast and outlive me. It just makes me happy to see my kids love and support each other.

In the same way, our Heavenly Parents want us to love each other as well as love Them. Our Heavenly Parents aren't looking for transactional relationships, either with Them or between Their children. They delight in our relationships of love for each other as well as our love for Them.

Today's society is fraught with zero-sum-game thinking, which means that the only way for me to win is for you to lose. The sum of my gain or loss and your gain or loss equals zero. It is a contractual relationship where you get yours, I get mine, and that's it. Then it quickly devolves into fighting over limited resources. That adversarial relationship is divisive because someone's going to win and someone's going to lose, and everyone is keeping score. You know what happens to the guy who loses? He spends the rest of his life seeking revenge, saying, "I've been beaten, and now I'm going to get you back." In a zero-sum game, no win ever lasts. It's always contested, and it continues to be contested into the future. There is no healing; there is no abundance. None. It's not possible.

Even if the relationship is adversarial, we need to find the human values that allow for abundance so that we can see each other, seek common ground, and figure out how to literally find a win-win, without relationship scorekeeping. The only way to win is in a spirit of abundance, as both sides say, "I don't want to spend the rest of my life trying to battle and beat you back. We've got to win together." That is the way of the track of abundance, the nontransactional track, the law of love.

On the finishing track, we can seek to heal the world and heal ourselves as a by-product. This track is the track of perpetuity: love leading to healing, which leads to more love. When I realized this, it unlocked for me what the gospel was about. Before that realization, the gospel was all theoretical. I loved the idea of certain things about the gospel, but all of a sudden, the gospel became very practical. This is how it works—this is how you actually DO the gospel in your life, by applying the concept of abundant thinking embedded in the law of love.

COACH BILL WALSH—A REVOLUTIONARY ABUNDANT THINKER

The spirit of abundance versus a zero-sum mentality makes me think of Coach Bill Walsh. When I joined the San Francisco 49ers in 1987, he was already world famous because he had won two Super Bowls. Often fame, power, and money are great corruptors. When you land on top of the heap, sometimes your behavior completely changes. But Bill Walsh was different.

He was known as a genius, far ahead of his time—generations ahead. He had flaws, as we all do, but he was an enlightened man. Bill changed the way the offense was played, but the changes went much deeper. Bill was the one that started to talk about the holistic nature of each person on the team: their mental health, their spiritual health, how they ate, how they trained. This was way before anyone ever started thinking about this, especially in football. Bill knew that he and the team were going to be beneficiaries of this incredibly progressive way to coach, teach, and play football.

I came in the middle of that, right at the apex, and I knew that this was not just going to be a five- or seven-year thing. It was going to be a generational thing. After I joined the team, on my very first day, I noticed that Bill had somebody walking around with him with a camera on his shoulder, taping everything Bill was saying.

Think about the fame and the notoriety that Bill already had. As I watched the crew taping this genius coach, my instinct was, well, they must be doing some kind of documentary, maybe for a Bill Walsh Museum, something like "a day in the life."

Over time I realized that Bill was creating a repository of everything that he knew: all the proprietary knowledge that led to Super Bowl victories, fame, and fortune. He was recording the highly secretive playbooks and offensive installations, his speeches, every time he talked to the team, his coaching out at practice—essentially his life's work at the apex of his fame, notoriety, and power. Not at the end of his career, not as a last generous act as a head coach, not just before he passed away. He did it while he was still coaching. He put this together because he wanted to hand it to his assistant coaches who were leaving for head coaching jobs, even knowing he was going to see these coaches playing against him in the future.

Imagine if Apple took all their secrets and just handed them out, knowing that people were going to come back and compete against them using this incredible knowledge.

Bill chose to do that. When assistant coach Mike Holmgren left the 49ers to become the head coach of the Packers, Bill handed him this toolkit: all of this material in paper, audio, and video, all collated and presented in a perfect way for someone to use.

On the way out the door, the last thing Bill said to Mike was, "Well, I'll see you in the championship game"—meaning that if you use this, you'll be a champion. And four years later, the Packers actually were in the championship game against us and beat us.

Bill told me one day that he started this toolkit because he had minority coaches that were not getting NFL head coaching jobs. This was before the Rooney rule in the NFL, which now requires that a certain number of minority candidates must be interviewed for any head coaching job. Bill was way ahead of that. He wanted his assistant coaches to break that NFL glass ceiling as qualified minority candidates. His effort to document his knowledge was founded on giving them the opportunity to be head coaches. The love that he had for others was ennobling, empowering.

What goes through a man's mind at the height of his worldly glory and power? To make a kit of proprietary knowledge and hand it out, knowing that it will be used against him? That's the spirit of love, without transaction, without expectation of anything in return.

That's the smaller part of the story. The bigger part of the story is that this toolkit has now been passed down through generations. As I travel around the league now on Monday nights as a sports commentator, I can take an inventory: I think well over half of all the teams in the NFL are heavily influenced by this toolkit, as either direct or indirect descendants of his coaching tree.

Before Bill Walsh, it was difficult to see any sense of partnership between management and players. Bill closed that canyon. He made us his partners. In the spirit of abundance, he made his future competitors his partners as well. The abundance that came out of that act is overwhelming.

What if everyone could be excellent? Bill was already a Hall of Fame coach. But what if everyone could be a Hall of Fame coach? What if every team could be as good as we were? It's an incredible thought.

It's not a bad thing to have proprietary knowledge and use it to your benefit. This is a very competitive, capitalistic world. There is a lot of money to be made. There is a lot of power to be claimed, and there is a lot of success to be found in zero-sum thinking. This is the norm: there are finite resources and we're going to fight over them. There will be a winner and a loser. And the winner is the vanquisher, and the loser is, well, the loser. Even when somebody wins in that zero-sum scenario, they don't actually win, because the vanquished, the person who's been beaten, never forgets. They know that the win has been taken from their hide. And so now you don't have a solution or a final victory because no one's ever satisfied. It's going to be a battle back until they get their piece of your hide—until they get their revenge.

There is no abundance in that situation. There can't be. There is no spirit of what we're trying to do *together*. It's just winners and losers. Football could be a zero-sum game. In fact, it was, and still is in many places. Bill single-handedly changed the nature of the game to where you started to see the spirit of abundance: one plus one equals three.

Our spirits expand when we think abundantly, versus the contracting nature of always watching your back to see if someone is taking advantage of you.

THE PREPARATORY LAW: MERIT-BADGE THEOLOGY

At its root, zero-sum thinking is self-interested. While we usually think of selfishness as a bad thing, there is an element of self-interest even in some of the more righteous things that we do. There are gradations of selfishness.

For instance, the law of Moses lists things to do to show righteousness and devotion to God. That's the preparatory law: doing something righteous for credit. As humans we love to be told that we're good. We love to feel special.

It's merit-badge theology. Boy Scouts and Girl Scouts are wonderful organizations, teaching incredibly important and useful principles. Young men and women are given tasks to hone their skills and to show their levels of service for credit. There are merit badges to earn, advancements to achieve, and ceremonies to show progress. As kids receive these merit badges and move up the ranks, they get a sense of service. People are benefitted, and they become more skilled. But at the root can be an element of self-interest. Some kids seek the public and private rewards of being a high-ranking scout.

This merit-badge thinking belongs to the preparatory law, which is just that—preparatory. It's good as far as it goes. But if we stay stuck in the preparatory law, sooner or later we discover that there is always more to do to prove our righteousness. We think it's good for us and for society and it's what God wants.

If I'm not careful, my spirituality ends up as essentially this sash with merit badges that show that I've done all these things. In doing those things, I'm proving to myself, to God, and to anyone else who sees my sash that I've done the work. That's not bad, but it's preparation, a platform to build a solid foundation, not an end in itself. That's because there is always more to prove as I seek this perfection. So many people have broken themselves over that, throwing themselves against the rocks of perfection. It's not that I stop striving to be better, but that I try to think less about myself (even my quest for perfection) and try to think more of others.

When I'm on the preparatory track, absorbed in merit-badge theology, I'm focused on the reward. Why would I do these hard things, whether merit requirements or covenant-keeping, if I'm not going to get credit for it?

What happens next is further "othering," as I think I have become an elite, elect person with special rewards, looking down on those who are less than I am. Elitism has infiltrated our culture in a dastardly way. If I remain self-focused, even on the track to the highest goal to be like God, the very fact of being self-focused will keep me from actually achieving my goal.

SODOM: GROTESQUE TREATMENT OF THE POOR AND STRANGERS[3]

A horrific example of self-focused obedience while simultaneously looking down on others comes from Genesis. Remember the city of Sodom that was consumed by fire raining down from heaven? The Lord explained why the city was destroyed in Ezekiel 16:49 (in addition to sexual violence, including toward Lot's guests and daughters, as outlined in Genesis 18–19):

> Behold, this was the iniquity of thy sister Sodom, pride, fulness of bread, and abundance of idleness was in her and in her daughters, neither did she strengthen the hand of the poor and needy.

---

3 Thanks to theologian Derek Knox of BeyondtheBlockPodcast.com for this insight (episode 128, October 25, 2021).

I often wondered what kind of pride and neglect of the poor would result in complete destruction of a city. Chapter 19 of the book of Jasher[4] explains what the people of Sodom were doing. Here's one example among many in that chapter:

> And when a poor man came to their land they would give him silver and gold, and cause a proclamation in the whole city not to give him a morsel of bread to eat, and if the stranger should remain there some days, and die from hunger, not having been able to obtain a morsel of bread, then at his death all the people of the city would come and take their silver and gold which they had given to him. And those that could recognize the silver or gold which they had given him took it back. (Jasher 19:8–9; sacred-texts.com/chr/apo/jasher/19.htm)

Do you get what's happening here? The people of Sodom would give money to the starving person because they were commanded to give to the poor. But first they would write their names on the coins. Then, because there was no commandment that they actually had to sell the person bread, they let him starve to death. When he died, they took their coins back. The people of Sodom had plenty of food ("fulness of bread," says Ezekiel 16:49). But they used their prosperity to mock the poor to death, literally.

This is beyond comprehension, this nefarious behavior to keep

---

4 While not canonized, the book of Jasher is defined in the Bible Dictionary: "Jasher, book of: (Josh. 10:13; 2 Sam. 1:18.) An early collection of Jewish national songs and stories of deeds of valor, put together about the time of Solomon."

the commandment while completely losing track of what the commandment was really intended to do. It's the ultimate sin of transaction, the ultimate self-interest: to obey the law to the degradation of everyone, including yourself. That kind of obedience without love is an extreme example of strict obedience gone haywire.

PHARISEES, SADDUCEES, AND THE PURPOSE OF THE LAW

When Christ came, His greatest rebukes were directed to those that were the most "righteous" (see Matthew 23:1–39). Yet the Pharisees and Sadducees[5] sat there every day thinking to themselves, *How can I be more righteous? How can I obey God's commandments better? I don't seek unrighteousness. I'm not looking to be evil at all. I'm doing what God told me to do!* But seeking for self-interested righteousness became absurd at some point.

The law of Moses was a series of things for people to do, intended to remind them of the Savior—the sacrifice of the unblemished firstborn male lamb, the blood painted on the doorposts for protection, etc. These are meaningful symbolic actions for people to take, pointing forward to the Atonement of Jesus Christ. But some

---

5 None of this is critical of Judaism itself, but of those particular Jewish leaders in Jesus's day that He scolded in Matthew 23: those who practice regulations to excess. Jesus Himself was a Jew. Even the Jewish historian Josephus [37–100 CE] commented on how many Jewish sects existed in his day. The Apostle Paul was a Pharisee (see Bible Dictionary, "Paul"). He had been doing what he thought God required, including participating in the martyrdom of Stephen (see Acts 8:1), until his eye-opening experience in Acts 9. If individuals live up to the light and knowledge they receive, the Atonement of Jesus Christ will cover them.

Pharisees and Sadducees in Jesus's time lost focus on where the law was pointing—to the Savior—because they focused on the law itself. Obedience became just a list of things to get done so that they could show their love for a good cause.

Over generations, the law became so rigid and so deeply embedded in their lives that it just didn't make sense anymore, such as literally counting steps on the Sabbath. The law became so prescriptive that the principle was lost to them, to the point that they couldn't even see the living Savior in front of them. He was the whole point of the law to which they went such lengths to obey! That tells you how far the observance of the law had rotted because of its self-focus. The Pharisees and Sadducees had gotten way off course trying too hard to follow it.

If we aren't careful, exact obedience to law can amount to nothing more than seeking a transactional relationship with the Divine. God asks me to be obedient. When I am, I receive righteousness and blessings. But if my obedience is only about seeking blessings, it will rot over time because of self-focus. It's all about what I can get, not what I can give to God or anyone else. Just like the Pharisees and Sadducees, I could spend all my life seeking righteousness and miss Jesus Christ standing right in front of me.

The biggest thing that is missing is love.

5

MORONI 7:
THE LAW OF LOVE ILLUMINATED

In my sixteen years of teaching Sunday School to adults, I've always been drawn to Moroni 7 in the Book of Mormon. Think of it: the prophet Moroni at the end of his life, the last survivor of the Nephite nation in the Americas, writing down his father Mormon's words. As the last Nephite alive, Moroni chose for his final act to be writing this down—and who knows who would read it? He so beautifully pounds out the overarching law of love, described as charity:

> None is acceptable before God, save the meek and
> lowly in heart; and if a man be meek and lowly in heart,
> and confesses by the power of the Holy Ghost that Jesus is
> the Christ, he must needs have charity; for if he have not
> charity he is nothing; wherefore he must needs have char-
> ity. And charity suffereth long, and is kind, and envieth
> not, and is not puffed up, seeketh not her own, is not easily
> provoked, thinketh no evil, and rejoiceth not in iniquity

but rejoiceth in the truth, beareth all things, believeth all things, hopeth all things, endureth all things. Wherefore, my beloved brethren, if ye have not charity, ye are nothing, for charity never faileth. Wherefore, cleave unto charity, which is the greatest of all, for all things must fail—But **charity is the pure love of Christ, and it endureth forever**; and whoso is found possessed of it at the last day, it shall be well with him. **Wherefore, my beloved brethren, pray unto the Father with all the energy of heart, that ye may be filled with this love,** which he hath bestowed upon all who are true followers of his Son, Jesus Christ; that ye may become the sons of God; that when he shall appear we shall be like him, for we shall see him as he is; that we may have this hope; that we may be purified even as he is pure. Amen. (Moroni 7:44–48; emphasis added)

Of course, the word "charity" here in Moroni 7 doesn't just mean giving to the poor. Charity is the law of love. To me, Moroni 7 is the stake in the ground where the law of love is taught and what it really means. That whole chapter reads as if it were personal. Moroni 7 just sings. And once I began to understand the law of love in Moroni 7, I saw that everything the Savior ever said in the New Testament and the Book of Mormon just sings too. With almost every lesson I teach, no matter what the subject is, when I layer on the law of love, it just sings in a different way.

The word "love" in "pure love of Christ" doesn't have to be romantic love, or even love for family or friends or people that I like. In any context, even with tough people in business or with an enemy that has harmed me, the law of love still works. In those contexts I can interchange the word "love" with respect, understanding, being willing to try to stand in another's shoes to seek empathy, or being willing to look at another's history and why and how they got here to this place. That's love to me. It doesn't have to be warm fuzzy feelings. Love is an action word. It's an intent to find healing, to see another as fully human, a child of the Divine, no matter what is going on between us. That kind of love is empowering and ennobling.

The word "pure" in "pure love" is intentional too. The law of love has to be pure, unmuddied by any sense of transaction or thought of "what's in it for me?," whether deposits in some celestial obedience account, or blessings that I seek, or even good feelings or peace that I want. All those things may come, but ironically, only if I don't seek them—only when my intent is purely to bless others. Pure love is simply love for its own sake, a true desire for the healing of others. The law of love can't be fooled, not even by hiding a selfish motive under an altruistic one. I may not be able to love with that kind of purity all the time, but that's what is in my heart. I only desire the healing of others. It's the direction I am headed.

These insights about the law of love in Moroni 7 are even more impressive when we understand where the author Mormon was coming from, as explained by John Bytheway:

> [The prophet] Mormon's life was filled with war. My dad's two years [in the military] deeply affected him. He was at Iwo Jima, with 7,000 American men lost and 20,000 wounded. Dad watched some of that through his binoculars as an eighteen-year-old. It deeply affected

him—[just] two years [at war]. But Mormon was a general since he was 16 [to at least age] 73. This battle-hardened general—what got him through all that? His whole life at war? Imagine him saying this: "Charity is the pure love of Christ. . . . Wherefore, my beloved brethren, pray unto the Father with all the energy of heart, that ye may be filled with this love, which he hath bestowed upon all who are true followers of his Son, Jesus Christ" (Mormon 7:47–48). (*Five Scriptures That Will Help You Get Through Almost Anything* [Salt Lake City: Deseret Book, 2002], track 9)

Somehow Mormon lived through a lifetime of war and still understood this law of love from such a deep place. I think Mormon is saying that these monumental teachings about charity also applied to his life experience on the battlefield, as impossible as that sounds. For me, those teachings also apply to battlefields in football, business, and even relationships. The teachings of Moroni 7 apply in every situation, in every life circumstance. The law of love is undefeated.

If I find it hard to get to this place of pure love, Moroni promises that I can "pray unto the Father with all the energy of heart, that [I] may be filled with this love" (Moroni 7:48). Sister Chieko Okazaki explained how this works: "The reason 'charity never faileth' (1 Corinthians 13:8) is because we aren't in charge of the supply department. Love comes from our Heavenly Father and Jesus Christ, spilling over into our own hearts until we simply brim over with love into the lives of others" (*Lighten Up* [Salt Lake City: Deseret Book, 1993]).

Beyond the preparatory law, rooted in zero-sum thinking and self-interest, is the higher law of love and the spirit of abundance. The law of love says that in your relationships with others, including Deity or other humans, you seek no transaction. In those relationships you seek only the good of others and their glory and their goodness and their healing, with no thought of what you could get back.

1 CORINTHIANS 13—THE LAW OF LOVE ACCORDING TO PAUL

What is interesting about Moroni 7 is that it was written around 400 CE in the Americas, but it sounds a whole lot like 1 Corinthians 13, written around 53–54 CE to the Greeks in Corinth. Moroni didn't have Paul's letters. But clearly this was important enough to God that these concepts were revealed to both of these prophets, in both the Old World and the New World.

A lot of the concepts in these two chapters overlap, but Paul adds this interesting observation: "When I was a child I spake as a child, I understood as a child, I thought as a child: but when I became a man, I put away childish things" (1 Corinthians 13:11). Paul is reinforcing the concept of moving beyond the preparatory law, the merit-badge theology, to this higher, holier law of love.

Sister Anne C. Pingree agrees. She's a former counselor in the Relief Society General Presidency. She said:

> Unlike the process of growing up physically, we will not mature spiritually until we *choose* to "put away childish things." We "put away childish things" as we choose to

become Christlike and serve others as He would have us do. Today, as the Church grows in 170 nations throughout the earth, *determined service to others,* even in difficult circumstances, is required of those who truly desire "to grow up unto the Lord" (Helaman 3:21). ("To Grow Up unto the Lord," *Ensign,* May 2006; emphasis in original)

WOUNDED HEALERS: IN GIVING WE RECEIVE

The irony of so many things in the gospel, but of the law of love in particular, is this: losing any thought of transaction and having your thoughts become wholly other-focused is the only way to actually receive back for yourself! The people I know that naturally live in this space are always the most balanced, whole, happy humans. They receive back the very thing that we all seek. Lose your life and you'll find it (see Matthew 10:39; 16:25). As I seek healing for others, I am healed myself, exactly as the Savior said.

This also means that we don't have to be healed first in order to heal others. In fact, we *can't* be healed ourselves *until* we heal others. That means that we are all **wounded healers**, seeking to heal others and thereby becoming whole ourselves. President Henry B. Eyring said, "We must notice the tribulation of others and try to help. **That will be especially hard when we are being sorely tested ourselves.** But we will discover as we lift another's burden, even a little, that our backs are strengthened and we sense a light in the darkness" ("Tested, Proved, and Polished," *Ensign,* Nov. 2020).

Moroni 7 says it too: verses 3 and 4 mention "the peaceable followers of Christ" and "your peaceable walk with the children of men." That whole chapter about the law of love results in peace—the kind of heart-deep peace we all seek, "no matter what is happening or not happening in our lives," as President Russell M. Nelson said ("Joy and Spiritual Survival," *Ensign*, Nov. 2016).

That's why the law of love is so wonderful—because it sends me away from myself. It doesn't tell me to quit trying to be better; it just asks me to stop thinking about myself.[1] I stop being so motivated to be perfect, thinking about how I need to measure up, and start focusing more on how I can try to heal others. That's the secret. In striving to heal others, I myself am healed. In a place of great personal challenge or anything else, I go seek someone else's healing and God starts to make a way out for me. It's just an incredible power.

An ancient parable illustrates this idea of wounded healer:

> There is an old Chinese tale about the woman whose only son died. In her grief, she went to the holy man and said, "What magic do you have to bring my son back to life?" He said to her, "Fetch me a mustard seed from a home that has never known sorrow. We will use it to drive the sorrow out of your life." The woman set off at once. She came to a splendid mansion and said, "I am looking for a home that has never known sorrow. Is this such a place?" They told her, "You've certainly come to the wrong place," and began to describe the tragic things that had befallen

---

1 "That day I had prayed for such a miracle to come instead of praying for how well I might do my part [serving others]. I prayed that the people would feel the Lord's love through my loving service" (Henry B. Eyring, "Bless in His Name," *Liahona*, May 2021).

them. The woman stayed to comfort them, then went on her search. Wherever she turned, in hovels and in palaces, she found sadness and misfortune. Ultimately, she became so involved in ministering to other people's grief that she forgot her quest for the magical mustard seed, never realizing that it had in fact driven the sorrow out of her life. (Harold S. Kushner, *When Bad Things Happen to Good People* [New York: Schocken Books, 1981])

Ann Madsen, former BYU instructor, told this tender story:

> Our youngest daughter, when she was about two years old, caught her hand in our old Ironrite[2] as the motor was on and the roller was rolling. Her tiny hand was badly friction burned. As I heard her cry and ran to free her hand and gather her up in my arms, I wept as I saw the wound and blamed myself for her pain. I rushed her to a basin and ran cold water over the burn, all the time sobbing until I became aware that she wasn't crying but was wiping away my tears and whispering, "Don't cry, Mommy. Look, I'll kiss it better." And she did. So can we. ("Jesus, the Very Thought of Thee," BYU Women's Conference address, 1997)

Even a two-year-old can be a wounded healer. She cared more about her mother's pain than her own. Her natural sense of love for the other—in this case, her mom—is where the healing is, resulting

---

2 An Ironrite is an electric rotary mangle iron, popular in the 1950s, with two rollers that press the fabric smooth.

in her own pain being diminished. That is, in seeking others' healing, we too are healed. The law of love is boundless. Its healing force, its selfless nature can come from any direction at any time, even from the example of a two-year-old.

FORCING RIGHTEOUSNESS: AGENCY AND THE LAW OF LOVE

In many ways, the law of love is rooted in agency as a bedrock, fundamental principle. We are injured by the misuse of agency, both self-inflicted and inflicted by others. Let's back up and look at agency in context.

Our Heavenly Parents—our Mother and Father in Heaven—have bodies, parts, and passions. Their hearts beat in sympathy with ours. We lived with Them as spirits before we chose to come to earth and take a body. We are eternal, divine beings and can choose to eventually return to live with Them.

Before our birth, when we lived as spirits with our Heavenly Parents, there was a Council in Heaven (see Moses 4:1–4). Carol Lynn Pearson describes what happened there beautifully in her song "I Have a Plan" from the musical *My Turn on Earth:*

> Satan: "I have a plan. It will save every man. **I will force them to live righteously.** They won't have to choose, not one we will lose. . . . Any problems and pain will not be. No wars and no strife, a wonderful life. Nobody needs to be free. Let me take care of you. If you follow me, I promise that not one soul will be lost. I will see to it personally that you are all taken care of and return here

without difficulty. You won't have to choose, and give all the glory to me."

Notice the false doctrine from Satan, the "father of all lies" (Moses 4:4). Here's Satan making a promise he can't deliver. Satan can't force us into heaven. It just wouldn't work. Satan sought to destroy our agency, which might just as easily mean we would never be ALLOWED to live righteously. Satan is "a liar from the beginning" (Doctrine and Covenants 93:25).

Here's Jesus's response in the song:

> Jesus: "I have a plan. It is better for man. Each will have to decide what to be. In choosing I know, you'll learn and you'll grow. . . . Each must learn to obey, if like Father and Mother we be. It's true that if you follow Me there will be dangers, difficulties, perhaps even wars and bloodshed, for you will be free to choose them if you wish. I cannot do everything for you. No one can, no one should. We must have the opportunity to choose, and there must be the possibility of wrong choices, to discover the powers within us, and not look continually to someone else. **To use our own agency: this is growth**, and growth must be. Follow Me, and Father, the glory to Thee." (Carol Lynn Pearson and Lex de Azevedo, "I Have a Plan," *My Turn on Earth* [Salt Lake City: Deseret Book, 1977]; emphasis added)

The Fall was a plan to allow us to be more like God. Choosing to take a body meant we could learn better how to love, trust, and be educated by painful and soul-stretching experiences, both bitter and sweet.

Our Heavenly Parents want to exalt the entire human family as They see us grow in our capacity to heal from woundedness and be redeemed from death. Their firstborn son Jesus Christ is the essential piece in this plan. We needed a Savior to deliver us. The whole plan is predicated on Jesus Christ and His sacrifice, redeeming us and opening the door for us to take this mortal journey toward eternal life. Without a Savior, we would be stuck forever as spirit children—incomplete and immature. We couldn't progress. We would be stuck on the dead-end track toward an eternity of nothingness.

When we came to this earth, the Savior called us to join Him as saviors with a little *s*: mentioned in Obadiah 1:21 ("saviours on mount Zion") and Doctrine and Covenants 103:9–10 ("For they were set to be a light unto the world, and to be the saviors of men; And inasmuch as they are not the saviors of men, they are as salt that has lost its savor"). Whenever we reach out to others without expectation of return, we are joining Christ in His exalting work, becoming "little-*s*" saviors.

In addition to being our Savior, Jesus is the great Healer. He has the capacity to heal everything—all the misuse of agency in our lives, both at our own hands and at the hands of others.

It's tempting to try to force others to live righteously according to our definition of righteousness. But that's Satan's plan! Not only do people rebel against being forced, but that plan simply doesn't work. I can force someone to keep the commandments, but I can't force them to become Christlike in their hearts. I can force someone to do the actions that earn them the righteousness merit badge, but they don't learn the Christlike qualities that the righteousness merit badge was intended to teach. It is the same for myself: if someone just gives me the checklist to earn the badge, I can goal-set my way down the list and never change my heart. The point was never the badge; it's the change of heart: learning to think as our Heavenly Parents think, and love as They love.

SATAN/OPPOSITION VS. GOD'S POWER

Never forget that God is categorically more powerful than Satan. One day my daughter said, "Dad, I don't like this Satan guy. It makes me really uncomfortable to talk about this person that can come and get me, you know?" I understood.

But remember, Satan's power is to bruise, but Jesus's power is exponentially greater (see Genesis 3:15, footnote c). Satan can bruise you to pieces, but you have access to so much more power through Christ. So whenever you feel a negative influence in your life, just know that you can crush its head. You can just step on it. Think about the relative power between bruising and crushing: it's not a fair fight. God wins every time. Through exercising your agency, you can choose to be on God's team and access divine power to crush opposition. The law of love is undefeated.

"One of the ways Satan wants us to manipulate others is by dwelling upon and even exaggerating the evil in the world," said Elder Dieter F. Uchtdorf ("Perfect Love Casteth Out Fear," *Ensign*, May 2017). He continued, "I don't believe God wants His children to be fearful or dwell on the evils of the world. . . . It is true that fear can have a powerful influence over our actions and behavior. But that influence tends to be temporary and shallow. Fear rarely has the power to change our hearts, and it will never transform us into people who love what is right and who want to obey Heavenly Father."

On the preparatory track, I call that tempting power Satan. On the finishing track, I call it opposition. Remember that Father Lehi said there must be "opposition in all things" (2 Nephi 2:11). Opposition is an opportunity, because I need opposition as well as a body and agency in order to make choices. That's the way I grow: by making choices. Opposition is better described as simply part of the plan, a polishing force, more than a terrible, frightening being who is personified as Satan. President Mark L. Pace, Sunday School General President, explained it this way at the 2021 BYU Women's Conference opening session:

> It would not be much of a test or a challenge without opposition of some kind. Without opposition, choice is meaningless. Opposition gives us the traction that moves us forward. ("Navigating Trials with Faith and Optimism," 2021 BYU Women's Conference, April 29, 2021)

Opposition is there for a purpose, and we need not empower it beyond its scope. Oddly, that actually frees me. I become fearless.

EVE—THE HEROINE IN THE GARDEN OF EDEN

I think that Eve understood these principles and the need for this education through agency and opposition and a body. With those elements in place, through the science of centropy, we can find perpetuity. I'm so grateful for our unique understanding of Eve. As far as I know, ours is the only church that understands Eve as the heroine of the Garden of Eden story. She was human—she was not God—so she was looking through this filter of limited understanding and opposition. Yet she had the inspiration to envision an ennobling, wondrous world beyond what she could see. I think Adam was satisfied with life in the garden, but Eve saw a greater good. I think she was able to discern that beyond the rigor of earth life ahead lay the grand glory of the whole scope of the plan of salvation.

Sometimes we think of suffering as the result of a flawed system. But what if suffering is the point—what if it IS the system?

Elder Bruce C. Hafen spoke about Elder Neal A. Maxwell and his suffering:

> After Elder Maxwell learned he had the leukemia that eventually took his life, he said, "I should have seen it coming." Why? Because ever since [his military service in] Okinawa he had wanted to become a fully consecrated follower of Jesus—no matter what the price. And the more he desired the gift of charity—to love as Christ loves—the more he sensed how dear the price might be. Christ's love is so deep that He took upon Himself the sins and afflictions of all mankind. Only in that way could He both pay for our sins and empathize with us enough to truly succor us—that is, run to us—with so much empathy that we can have complete confidence that He fully understands our sorrows. So, to love as Christ loves means we

will somehow taste suffering ourselves—for the love and the affliction are but two sides of the same coin. Only by experiencing both sides can we understand and love other people with a depth that even approaches Christ's love. ("A Disciple's Journey," BYU devotional, February 5, 2008)

Some people suffer just to suffer, but others use their suffering to become more Christlike, giving their suffering a purpose. Christ can give us "beauty for ashes" (Isaiah 61:3). He says, in effect, "I can alchemize anything that happens in this world to your healing, to your benefit, if you give Me a chance. That means all the suffering and anything else—the worst of the worst." This applies both to suffering innocently at the hands of others as Christ did and to our suffering for our own mistakes. Paul wrote to the Hebrews: "God . . . provided some better things for them through their sufferings, for without sufferings they could not be made perfect" (Joseph Smith Translation, Hebrews 11:40).

At the same time, those statements give us no license to inflict useless suffering on others. Ever.

When Christ alchemizes the worst of the worst, you have the chance to be a special agent in that area. That is, when Christ alchemizes the ashes of abuse, you become an expert in abuse. When Christ alchemizes the ashes of substance abuse, you become an expert in addiction. You are now a special agent in that thing, because Christ alchemized it for your good and the good of others. He needs modern-day experts in all this stuff to help all His children, no matter what challenges they face, each one paying it forward.

We're not here because of a broken system. This life is not a mistake. Agency, opposition, the challenges of a body, the rigor of our lives—if we think of it in terms of growth and special-agent training, then even the most brutal, difficult things are a little easier to bear.

THE INTERSECTION OF INSPIRATION AND AGENCY

The law of love is at the intersection of inspiration and agency. That intersection is an incredible truth to our restored gospel, despite the human experience, the complexity, and the opaqueness. For me, inspiration is always shards and pieces and thoughts, but they can collect and grow and enlarge.

At the same time, the intersection of inspiration and agency is a messy place. Sometimes we don't hear clearly, or we do the wrong thing. Everyone does. That's the whole point. We need to be honest with ourselves that this messy process is the price of growth.

Agency has to be complete in the selfless, nontransactional effort. There is no compulsion in the gospel of Jesus Christ. I can't force anyone to do anything, no matter how badly I want it. I'm grateful for that because agency is how we grow. It's the freedom to live our own lives and the agency we recognize as this rootedness. The Qur'an says it this way: "There is no compulsion in religion. Had your Lord willed, everyone on earth would have believed. Shall *you* then force people to become believers?" (Qur'an, Al-Baqara 256; emphasis added).

We may want our children to choose certain things so we feel like good parents. Or we may want a loved one to choose sobriety so we can have peace of mind and build the family that we want. But that way of thinking is a transactional relationship. We do things for others or try to force them to do things that will give us what we want. In the end, we can only love others and support them as they figure out their lives for themselves (within boundaries—see page 151).

Certainly on the preparatory track, I can support my children to make good choices until their sense of self and understanding of consequences is sufficiently mature for them to make more choices on their own. But I can't hold their hand and walk with them on their own preparatory track forever. I can support them forever, sure. But sooner or later they have to make their own choices. The preparatory track, while good, doesn't take them or me where we want to be—that sustainable, perpetual place of abundance found in the finishing track, the law of love.

You cannot change what you do not love.[3] Heart-deep change doesn't come from either coercion or incentives. It can only come through love. This is the way Christ invites us to change our hearts: not by force or bribes, but by loving invitation, by attraction.

I can't save; Christ does that. I can't actually heal, but I can seek to provide space for Christ to heal. Fiona and Terryl Givens explain it this way:

> Christ's incomparable gift is his power and desire to heal us all as individuals, regardless of the nature of our wounds. This is at-one-ment. . . . Healing is the central

---

3 Much to my surprise, this quote from me is now on the walls of one of the buildings of the Red Barn Academy in Farmington, Utah (redbarnfarms .org). My friend Rich Haws founded this incredible organization as a vocational training school for men in recovery so they could learn farming as well as life skills through hard work in a supportive environment.

activity of his ministry in the New Testament and the Book of Mormon alike. . . . The damage wrought—to ourselves and to others—by what we call sin needs healing just as much as other forms of spiritual and emotional harm do. The most fruitful way of considering sin may not be to see it as an evil that leads to a hell from which we must be *saved* but rather as a wound that needs to be *healed*. ("Atonement: From Penal Substitution to Radical Healing—An Excerpt from *All Things New* by Terryl and Fiona Givens," faithmatters.org)

That's an astonishing thought that subtly but profoundly reshapes our understanding of sin and salvation: realizing that sin results in wounds in ourselves and others that need redemption through Christ's Atonement. That's the law of love in action.

TRANSFIGURED EYESIGHT

Another aspect of the law of love is this: in seeking others' healing, my eyes can be transfigured, and I can see other humans as God sees them. The promise is that in this nontransactional effort, with transfigured eyes, I can see the person in front of me as an eternal being with infinite potential.

I think of Elder Robert C. Gay, who spoke in general conference about his sister:

> A few years ago my older sister passed away. She had a challenging life. She struggled with the gospel and was never really active. Her husband abandoned their marriage

and left her with four young children to raise. On the evening of her passing, in a room with her children present, I gave her a blessing to peacefully return home. At that moment I realized I had too often defined my sister's life in terms of her trials and inactivity. As I placed my hands on her head that evening, I received a severe rebuke from the Spirit. I was made acutely aware of her goodness and allowed to see her as God saw her—not as someone who struggled with the gospel and life but as someone who had to deal with difficult issues I did not have. I saw her as a magnificent mother who, despite great obstacles, had raised four beautiful, amazing children. I saw her as the friend to our mother who took time to watch over and be a companion to her after our father passed away. During that final evening with my sister, I believe God was asking me, "Can't you see that everyone around you is a sacred being?" . . . From the Spirit's rebuke at my sister's bedside, I learned a great lesson: that **as we see as He sees**, ours will be a double victory—redemption of those we touch and redemption of ourselves. ("Taking upon Ourselves the Name of Jesus Christ," *Ensign*, Nov. 2018; emphasis added)

As Elder Gay spoke, I realized that when we see others deeply, transfiguratively, beyond today, beyond the challenges and the decisions that we might think are bad or good, we see them as eternal beings. That too is part of charity or the law of love. Moroni 7 begs us to start to do this, to be this.

In those charitable acts, that's how I receive. Just as the law of obedience has its own rewards, so does the law of love. The rewards of the law of love are perpetual, celestial, eternal. That's why Moroni 7 to me is something super special, because as I lay that lens on every speech, every scripture, everything that I read, I can sift through and find what feels more important, more useful, ennobling, perpetual.

Every day I can pray for inspiration: "Lord, tell me how to live the full measure of my life. What should I do?" I keep hearing back the same answer every time. "Live your religion. I told you. I told you how to act."

At first, I thought, "Live my religion? What do you think I'm doing?" But as the answer unfolded itself to me, I came to realize what God meant. It wasn't what I expected. It wasn't the checklist of commandments like I thought—in fact, it's the opposite of the self-focused checklist. It's about always being aware of others, seeking others' perspectives with gentleness, meekness, long-suffering, and love unfeigned. It's seeking a way to describe the joy I feel from the gospel. That's why I'm so energized by this law of love and by the restored gospel.

I feel like every human being should hear those ennobling, energizing things. What if I just walked up and down my hometown and knocked on doors and said, "Did you know that you're divine? that God bore our spirits and we're all divine?" They might close the door, but they're not going to say that's crazy or dumb or that it doesn't taste good or it's offensive. Regardless of what someone else does with it, even if they do nothing, it just puts a smile on their face. That's success. It's like Johnny Appleseed throwing seeds out there and not worrying about which ones sprout, just sowing seeds.

C. S. Lewis's famous quote comes into play here:

> It is a serious thing to live in a society of possible gods and goddesses, to remember that the dullest and most uninteresting person you can talk to may one day be a creature which, if you saw it now, you would be strongly tempted to worship. . . . It is in the light of these overwhelming possibilities, it is with the awe and the circumspection proper to them, that we should conduct all of our dealings with one another, all friendships, all loves, all play, all politics. There are no ordinary people. You have never talked to a mere mortal. It is immortals whom we joke with, work with, marry, snub, and exploit— immortal horrors or everlasting splendors. (*The Weight of Glory* [London: *Theology*, 1941])

When I truly see others as possible gods and goddesses, their success and their healing become more important to me than my bean-counting goals. Elder Dieter F. Uchtdorf told this story:

> I know of a stake where the leaders set some ambitious goals for the year. While the goals all looked worthwhile, they focused either on lofty and impressive declarations or on numbers and percentages.
>
> After these goals had been discussed and agreed upon, something began to trouble the stake president. He thought about the members of his stake—like the young mother with small children who was recently widowed. He thought about the members who were struggling with

doubts or loneliness or with severe health conditions and no insurance. He thought about the members who were grappling with broken marriages, addictions, unemployment, and mental illness. And the more he thought about them, the more he asked himself a humbling question: will our new goals make a difference in the lives of these members? He began to wonder how their stake's goals might have been different if they had first asked, "What is our ministry?"

So this stake president went back to his councils, and together they shifted their focus. They determined that they would not allow "the hungry, . . . the needy, . . . the naked, . . . the sick and the afflicted to pass by [them], and notice them not" (Mormon 8:39). They set new goals, recognizing that success with *these* new goals could not always be measured, at least not by man—for how does one measure personal testimony, love of God, or compassion for others? But they also knew that "**many of the things you can count, do not count. Many of the things you cannot count, really do count**" (attributed to Albert Einstein).

I wonder if our organizational and personal goals sometimes . . . look impressive from a distance but fail to address the real needs of our beloved fellowmen? If Jesus Christ were to sit down with us and ask for an accounting of our stewardship, I am not sure He would focus much on programs and statistics. What the Savior would want to know is the condition of our heart. He would want to know how we love and minister to those in our care, how we show our love to our spouse and family, and how we lighten their daily load. And the Savior would want to know how you and I grow closer to Him and to our Heavenly Father. ("On Being Genuine," *Ensign*, May 2015; emphasis added)

That transfigured eyesight applies to the way we see others, but it also applies to the way we see ourselves and even God. Back to Moroni 7, the last verse: "Wherefore, my beloved brethren, pray unto the Father with all the energy of heart . . . ; that ye may become the sons [and daughters] of God; that **when he shall appear we shall be like him, for we shall see him as he is;** that we may have this hope; that we may be purified even as he is pure" (Moroni 7:48; emphasis added).

To see that I really am like God, and that others are too? What I wouldn't give up to have that transfigured eyesight! Moroni 7 tells me it's possible through the law of love on the nontransactional, finishing track.

BUILDING ZION

I think about people in the city of Enoch (see Moses 7:68–69). Sure, they were righteous, but I don't think their righteousness took them to heaven. I think it was love that took them to heaven—because that's how it works. I think they couldn't have gotten to heaven any other way. The people of Enoch had to leave the entropic world because they were collectively living the higher law and couldn't be held any longer here on earth. That's how you can escape this world.

Many times I think about our Church, with 16 million of us and counting. If we sought nothing but healing of other humans, with missionaries out there teaching this healing spirit, that could be our highest calling, the full measure of our creation, seeking this centropic place. It's so subtle too because you can't seek it directly; you can only give it away. This has to be about each of us living this higher law, no matter who you are or where you are.

When we talk about a place of Zion or a church of Zion or a group of Zion, it can't just be full of obedient people. It has to be full of those that are living this higher law. That's why the law of love is so vital, because it's actually what we seek in our spiritual lives. We seek this place, we pray for this place, we hope for this place. But without a firm understanding of the law of love, we can't be there, because that place can't be earned. There is no righteousness merit badge that will get us in. Even if I'm thoughtful and faithful, even if I work hard (I mean *hard*), if I do it in a transactional mindset to achieve something, it's still me trying to earn my way into Zion.

Obedience is a wonderful thing, but it's a foundational thing, a platform. But living in perpetuity can't just be based on obedience, because obedience in the end is a transactional way of being: expecting the return compensation of God's love here in this world and eternal life in the world to come. As we seek this perpetual place, we need to firmly understand the law of love, this nontransactional way of being, and begin to live it.

How did Enoch do it? How did he achieve that higher law for

himself and lead his whole people to that centropic place? The scriptures give us this clue: "And the Lord spake unto Enoch, and said unto him: Anoint thine eyes with clay, and wash them, and thou shalt see. And he did so. And he beheld the spirits that God had created; and he beheld also things which were not visible to the natural eye" (Moses 6:35–36).

There it is! Right there! God gave Enoch transfigured eyesight, that ability to see deeply into the souls of others. And what was the result? "The Lord . . . told Enoch all the doings of the children of men; wherefore Enoch knew, and . . . stretched forth his arms, and his heart swelled wide as eternity" (Moses 7:41). When we see, *really* see others, our hearts swell as wide as eternity, right there with Enoch. That transfigured eyesight leads us to this higher law of love.

The Church is moving in this direction, implementing more principle-based vs. prescriptive programs in many ways. An example is moving beyond Personal Progress for girls and the Scouting programs for boys, with hundreds of set requirements, and implementing the Children and Youth program, in which they set their own goals, four at a time (intellectual, physical, spiritual, and social, based on Jesus's growth when He was a child, from Luke 2:52).

This trend away from prescriptive programs and toward principles goes back to Joseph Smith's statement. When a man asked Joseph how he governed so many people in Nauvoo, Illinois, "[Joseph] said that it was very easy to do that. 'How?' responded the gentleman; 'to us it is very difficult.' Mr. Smith replied, 'I teach them correct principles, and they govern themselves'" (John Taylor, in *Millennial Star*, [Liverpool, England, Nov. 15, 1851], 339).

It's messier, to be sure, but principle-based expression leads you to more of a nontransactional experience.

SHIFT IN PERCEPTION—MAYBE SUBTLE, BUT VITAL

The difference may be subtle and sometimes it's hard to see, but to me the idea of transactional and nontransactional relationships really helps me to understand. For some, it's a game-changer. For others, the difference between the two is small, nearly imperceptible. Think about two boats that leave the same port, going in the same direction but just a degree or two off course from one another. Four days out, they're going to be a long way apart.

Although this shift in perception to nontransactional relationships may be a subtle change in trajectory, clearly over time it can put us in a much different place. My experience is that this change is fundamental to our individual sense of theology and how we see our relationship with God. Elder Donald L. Hallstrom, formerly of the Presidency of the Seventy, says it like this:

> **Some have come to think of activity in the Church as the ultimate goal. Therein lies a danger.** It is possible to be active in the Church and less active in the gospel. Let me stress: activity in the Church is a highly desirable goal; however, it is insufficient. Activity in the Church is an outward indication of our spiritual desire. If we attend our meetings, hold and fulfill Church responsibilities, and serve others, it is publicly observed.
>
> By contrast, the things of the gospel are usually less visible and more difficult to measure, but they are of greater

eternal importance. ("Converted to His Gospel through His Church," *Ensign*, May 2012; emphasis added)

Our activity in the Church can be transactional: attending meetings, fulfilling callings, and even performing service, all so we can be publicly observed and show God our obedience. But the gospel itself is the nontransactional, less visible things. It's like we mistake the "form of godliness" for the "power thereof" (Joseph Smith—History 1:19). Or, as the Lord said to Isaiah, "This people draw near me with their mouth, and with their lips do honour me, but have removed their heart far from me" (Isaiah 29:13).

Sometimes I think to really keep the commandments you can't even have the self-satisfaction that you did something good. It makes me think of this scripture:

> Two men went up into the temple to pray; the one a Pharisee, and the other a publican. The Pharisee stood and prayed thus with himself, God, I thank thee, that I am not as other men are, extortioners, unjust, adulterers, or even as this publican. And the publican, standing afar off, would not lift up so much as his eyes unto heaven, but smote upon his breast, saying, God be merciful to me a sinner. I tell you, this man went down to his house justified rather than the other: for every one that exalteth himself shall be abased; and he that humbleth himself shall be exalted. (Luke 18:10–11, 13–14)

Two things I notice about this scripture: the first is about the publican (meaning a tax collector, despised by nearly everyone at that time). He is doing good things! He's in the temple, praying. But he is doing it in a humble way, not patting himself on the back, without a shred of self-satisfaction. In fact, the publican's only words are "God be merciful to me a sinner," while he's in the very act of performing these righteous actions.

In contrast, notice how the self-righteous Pharisee is praying: he "prayed thus with himself." Do I ever pray with myself instead of with God? Only by praying with heaven, not praying with myself, can I rise to what I am being called to do.

Some folks say to me, well, Steve, I've got things to do, people to take care of, bills to pay, you know, transactional things to get done; this airy stuff about the law of love is just a theory. My response is: I know there's a lot to get done in a day. Sometimes life comes at us in torrents. But living the law of love is not just another thing to do. It's how I start every day; it's how I engage the world. In that space, as I'm working through all the busy-ness, the law of love defines my relationships and how I think about other human beings and about God, in every interaction, every moment, every breath. While meeting the needs and the challenges and the entropy of the day, I can get distracted from my focus. It's all part of life, but then I get back into that mental and spiritual space. As I take care of all those ordinary things I have to get done while simultaneously staying in that space, the law of love defines my relationships and how I think about other human beings and about God. It calls me to a different kind of nontransactional relationship.

6

ENTERING A NONTRANSACTIONAL RELATIONSHIP WITH GOD

I seek to love God with my whole soul. But how can I show God my love? What does my love for God look like? It starts with obedience—but it doesn't end there.

Jesus Himself asked us to start with obedience: "If ye love me, keep my commandments" (John 14:15). Obedience is submission to God; it's surrender to His will. That's a wonderful way to begin to show my love for God. But in my obedience, I can get wrapped up in the checklist culture. I might be subtly looking for the reward—the blessings God has promised me for my obedience (see Doctrine and Covenants 82:10). I may get lost in simply doing the obedient actions without letting it change the way I love God, with a pure, nontransactional love.

Although no human remembers it, I imagine the rawness of that moment when each of us left the presence of our Heavenly Parents and came to earth and took a body. We completely surrendered to Them and Their plan, not exactly knowing what we were getting ourselves into, certainly not knowing what was going to happen in this life. As we were leaving the presence of our Heavenly Parents, I doubt that we were thinking, "How righteous am I? How am I doing so far?" I doubt we even asked those questions. I bet we were thinking, "Put me in, God—send me on my way to do what You would have me do on earth." Then we jumped off a cliff into mortality.

In this life, constantly evaluating our own righteousness is no more productive. It keeps us centered on ourselves and our "performance" instead of focusing on our love for God or for others. It's just like when we left our premortal life: now that we're here, we have to enter that same rawness of complete faith and total love for God, ready to do God's will, not really knowing where it leads, seeking nothing for ourselves.

Once we're ready to move to the finishing track, again it is Jesus Himself who told us what to do next. Just seven chapters after explaining to the disciples how to love Him ("If ye love me, keep my commandments" in John 14), Jesus explained the next step in how to show our love for Him:

> Lovest thou me more than these? [Peter] saith unto him, Yea, Lord; thou knowest that I love thee. He saith unto him, Feed my lambs. He saith to him again the second time, Simon, son of Jonas, lovest thou me? He saith unto him, Yea, Lord; thou knowest that I love thee. He saith unto him, Feed my sheep. He saith unto him the third time, Simon, son of Jonas, lovest thou me? Peter was grieved because he said unto him the third time, Lovest thou me? And he said unto him, Lord, thou knowest all

things; thou knowest that I love thee. Jesus saith unto him, Feed my sheep. (John 21:15–17)

Reaching for the higher level of nurturing and healing others—that's how Jesus asks us to show that we love Him. He asks us to demonstrate our love for Him by seeking to heal others. Paul's schoolmaster scripture applies here:

Is the law then against the promises of God? God forbid: for if there had been a law given which could have given life, verily righteousness should have been by the law. Wherefore **the law was our schoolmaster to bring us unto Christ.** (Galatians 3:21, 24; emphasis added)

Did you catch that? If the law of obedience could have given life, then complete righteousness could be accomplished with nothing more than obedience. But the law of obedience is the schoolmaster to bring us to Christ, whereas the law of love pulls obedience forward in a different way. Under the law of love, we remain obedient, but this time out of pure love for God and others, not for credit for ourselves.

Remember that feeling of rawness, jumping off the cliff into mortality, not knowing exactly what was coming but trusting in God? It's that same feeling when we show Jesus that we love Him by feeding His lambs. We can seek to do nothing but His will to heal others, not exactly knowing where He is leading us, but wanting to show our love for Him in this selfless, other-focused way.

President Harold B. Lee said it this way: "Just before the dedication of the Los Angeles Temple, I enjoyed an experience that I think was not a dream, but it must have been a vision. I seemed to have heard [a] voice say, 'If you want to love God, you have to learn to love and serve the people. That is the way you show your love for God'" ("Stand Ye in Holy Places," *Ensign*, May 1973).

STARTING AS AN OBEDIENT DISCIPLE, THEN BECOMING A PARTNER WITH GOD

As I mentioned, first God invites us onto the obedience track, then He invites us to greater and greater heights on the nontransactional, finishing track.

We begin by choosing to be God's obedient disciple, which is a subordinate position, like loving, good children in relationship with Heavenly Parents. Then those Parents invite us into a *partnership* with Them, so we can grow into a relationship in which we can receive the full measure of what our Heavenly Parents have. This astonishing doctrine was revealed through Joseph Smith again and again:

> As many as have loved me and kept my commandments . . . shall come forth . . . , to receive a crown of righteousness, and to be clothed upon, **even as I am, to be with me, that we may be one.** (Doctrine and Covenants 29:12–13; emphasis added throughout)

> They who dwell in his presence are the church of the Firstborn; and they see as they are seen, and know as they are known, having received of his fulness and of his grace;

And he makes them **equal in power, and in might, and in dominion.** (Doctrine and Covenants 76:94–95)

And he that receiveth my Father receiveth my Father's kingdom; therefore **all that my Father hath shall be given unto him.** (Doctrine and Covenants 84:38)

And then shall the angels be crowned with the glory of his might, and the saints shall be filled with his glory, and receive their inheritance and **be made equal with him.** (Doctrine and Covenants 88:107)

For if you keep my commandments you shall **receive of his fulness**, and be glorified in me as I am in the Father; therefore, I say unto you, you shall receive grace for grace. (Doctrine and Covenants 93:20)

[They] shall **inherit thrones, kingdoms, principalities, and powers, dominions, all heights and depths** ... ; and they shall pass by the angels, and the gods, which are set there, to their exaltation and glory in all things, as hath been sealed upon their heads. . . . Then shall they be gods, **because they have all power**, and the angels are subject unto them. Verily, verily, I say unto you, except ye **abide my law** ye cannot attain to this glory. (Doctrine and Covenants 132:19–21)

About that last part—"except ye abide my law"—what law might that be? Only the law of love can fill the full measure of this celestial partnership. It's full consecration: all for all. All that we have for all that our Heavenly Parents have. Instead of simply asking for obedient servants (a good place to start), They ask us to step up and be partners, loving as They love.

"GO TO THE BREAD"

My mentor Carol Burr was fantastic at this, showing her love for Jesus by caring for His lambs, whoever and wherever they might be, and entering into partnership with our Heavenly Parents and Their work. I met Carol through her cousins Gene and Claire Freedman, who were in my home ward in Connecticut. When I was preparing to leave for my anxiety-ridden freshman year at BYU, my parents told the Freedmans that they weren't sure I was going to make it and that I needed some support. The Freedmans told them about Carol, their cousin in Provo, mother of nine kids, and she was amazing.

Going to the Burrs' house the first time, even just the noise of the family made me feel right at home. Their house became my second home. I lived up there for a while. Carol and I really connected. The depth of her knowledge of the gospel was incredible, and her support and listening ear really helped me survive that first year away from home.

In her personal journey of discipleship, Carol had reached a point where she wanted to do nothing but God's will. She knew that God was in the details of her life, and she wanted God to lead her every moment. She had this constant prayer with every breath: *What can I do for Thee? Whom can I serve? How can I help?* Carol just wanted to free herself of anything else, not desiring anything for herself. That is consecration, right there.

Once, Carol was in the grocery store when she felt this inspiration come into her mind: *Go to the bread.* At first she thought, "Huh?" But she had learned to not question those feelings, so she went right over to the bread aisle. She noticed a certain woman with several children that seemed to be the reason why she was there. Carol started a conversation with her, saying, "I'm here at the bread and you're here too, and I feel like God has brought me here. Could you explain that to me?" The woman broke down right in the grocery store and told Carol that her husband had tried to steal the children and there was domestic abuse involved. She was in desperate need of support and didn't know what to do. She was stuck and couldn't figure out her next move.

With utmost kindness and gentleness, Carol found the woman a shelter where she could be safe and get some help. Carol brought the children to her own home for a few days while their mom could get things settled in the shelter. Carol explained to her own nine children, "Here are our new friends. They're going to stay with us for a while."

Carol's actions that day were nothing new: she did this often for people who needed a place to stay (including me). Her children were used to having their mom bring home extra new friends from time to time when there was a need that God called her to fill. In fact, Carol's daughter Susan said, "As kids, we would never ask who were the house guests or what were the circumstances. We just knew we had people at home that we needed to be friends with, people who needed to be loved."

God may not call us to bring home new friends or call us to

intervene in risky situations. But wherever God calls us, the principle is the same: Carol completely abandoned anything else in her life other than God's will, doing everything she could to be available for God's work. Then God could use her for an errand that needed to get done immediately, over in the bread aisle.

What if we could live our whole lives that way? A lifetime of living the law of love means seeking others' healing as we extend Jesus's Atonement into other people's lives, completely devoid of any expectation or transaction between us/God or us/others. Our only motivation is love.

When I think about what heaven must be like, it's where we have lost ourselves, and thereby we have become the full measure of who we can be. I think that's what Jesus meant when He said that when we lose ourselves, we find ourselves (see Luke 9:24). In our nontransactional relationship, as we seek to love God with all our hearts, laying our agency on the altar, consecrating all of our hopes for ourselves—in that kind of love for the Divine, we shouldn't be surprised if God sends us back out from the altar over to the bread aisle.

7

CHRIST, THE GREAT HEALER, CALLING US TO HEAL EACH OTHER

The highest call we can have is this law of love. Part of our fundamental doctrine is that we have chosen to come down and take a body to be tried and tested and to learn and grow in an educative round. And Christ is here to heal us, to provide an opportunity for us to grow and to be educated. He is the great Healer as we go through this process. His healing balm is what we all seek. What if other humans could carry this balm to you? What if we could carry it to others?

What is this balm? It is this nontransactional, other-focused healing with nothing sought in return. And in that act, essentially we are acting as Christ. We are doing His work.

Name a time that Christ said or did anything in order to seek something for Himself. If we're going to love like Christ, if we're going to love like our Heavenly Parents, it needs to be nontransactional.

When God said, "This is my work and my glory—to bring to

pass the immortality and eternal life of man" (Moses 1:39), where's the transaction? What does God get? Nothing. Our Heavenly Parents only seek our growth, healing, exaltation, and glory. Her North Star, His North Star, is us. Her mission, His mission, is to create glory for us.

If we're going to be like our Heavenly Parents, then we better learn to love like Them. And it becomes very obvious to me that Their kind of love is completely selfless. They receive glory through the focused effort of seeking our glory. As I try to become more like my Heavenly Parents, I am learning to love like Them by creating glory for others too. That becomes my motivation. I seek to make every decision using that as my standard: helping others to achieve their full measure.

One more time: the full measure of heaven can only come through other people. I can't get there on my own. God receives glory through our glory; we receive glory through others' glory. That's how it works.

Whether we make a terrible mistake or do something wonderful, our Heavenly Parents can use any experience to teach us, to help us grow, to help us become more like Them. We don't need to get off track looking for blessings we "deserve" for our obedience. We can keep the commandments for no other reason than that we love our Heavenly Parents, and we love our fellow humans, and we want to bring the Savior's healing to them.

That scripture—Moses 1:39—belongs to the finishing track, the nontransactional track. Other scriptures belong to the preparatory track, like Doctrine and Covenants 82:10: "I, the Lord, am bound when ye do what I say; but when ye do not what I say, ye have no promise." That's a transaction right there. And it's perfectly fine, once you understand which scripture belongs on which track.

As I said, God paved both tracks, and both have their place. But come on over to the finishing track—the higher, holier law of love— as soon as you can, so you can be about God's business of healing others, and thereby healing yourself.

THE ROOT OF HEALING IN JUST THE "HELLO"

What is the beginning of the healing we seek to bring to others? Most of the time it's a small kindness that is the first step, even if it takes years for the other person to warm up. Maybe it's a wave and a hello, a heartfelt spirit that brings the Spirit.

Growing up, I was assigned to an elderly man named Jim Bonner as my home teaching[1] companion. We had several families to visit and watch over. In Connecticut, with our congregation boundaries so spread out, it could take all day. When I was seventeen, I did not have all day to go home teaching. Sometimes we visited a family, and it would just be a knock on the door, and they would say, "No, we're fine, thanks, have a nice day." I would think, what a waste of time.

But Brother Bonner said to me, "Steve, the needs of people, you just never know. You have to go, you have to ask, you have to see. Visiting is so important because you have to see them, you have to knock on their door."

Brother Bonner told me about a family that he visited before we were companions. He stopped by over and over, and over and over

---

1 The program that preceded ministering.

again, and he would knock on the door, stand on the porch, and just say, "Hello, we want you to know we're here, we love you."

And they would say, "No, thanks. No, we don't want anything here."

They never told him not to come back, but they never invited him in, either. Month after month, Brother Bonner would stop by, and they would have the same one-minute conversation at the door.

One day the dad of the family called Jim because his wife had collapsed and he said, "I didn't know who to call, but I called you because you keep coming to my door. So when I needed somebody, I decided to call the guy that came to my door all the time." Jim rushed over and essentially saved the woman's life.

The root of the healing was in the hello, just the small kindness, for years. It was no more than that. I never forgot that lesson that Brother Bonner taught me. Now when I visit my ministering families, who don't always let me in either, I say, "If ever you need someone, I'm the one that says hello. I am here for you, whatever you need."

BEYOND THE "HELLO": CHRISTMAS DINNER WITH THE MONTANAS[2]

After the hello comes getting to know the person. Just getting acquainted with someone demystifies them and enables us to see the human being.

---

2 A version of this story appeared in *QB: My Life Behind the Spiral*, by Steve Young with Jeff Benedict (Boston/New York: Mariner Books/Houghton Mifflin Harcourt, 2016), 138.

Later I'll talk more about the awkwardness between San Francisco 49er quarterback Joe Montana and me (having two quarterbacks is uncomfortable, let me tell you). But in spite of all of the angst, it was never personal between us.

One year Joe asked me to come over for Christmas dinner. Back then I was single, and everyone was thinking, "Let's help Steve out." It was really cool of Joe to do, sharing part of his family's Christmas day with me. At Christmas dinner we were sitting at the table talking when Joe's daughter, who was probably around three years old, raised her hand. "Dad," she said. "Dad."

Joe kept talking to me. "Dad," she repeated. "Dad."

"What?" Joe said sweetly.

"Is this the guy we hate?" she asked innocently. It got real quiet, then everyone laughed. "No," Joe told her. "That was someone else."

It's an amusing memory, but there is a true principle here. It can be tempting to have negative feelings for a person or a group of people in the abstract. Once you meet them, it humanizes them, and you realize that we're all just regular people doing the best we can. We can do a world of good by stepping outside our ordinary comfort circles and meeting others, putting a human face on someone unfamiliar.

FOUR POWER WORDS

When we sit in that healing space, it's amazing what can happen. Doctrine and Covenants 121:41 gives us four power words to implement as we use the priesthood (which is defined as the power of God).[3] This instruction applies to women and their priesthood authority as well, which explains why these four power words are right in the scriptures, not in some ecclesiastical priesthood leadership manual. In the women's session of general conference in 2019, President Nelson reminded women of "the priesthood power with which you [women] have been endowed" ("Spiritual Treasures," *Ensign*, Nov. 2019). In the temple, in our highest, most sacred places, men and women are equal, with the exact same priesthood power. So those verses in Doctrine and Covenants 121:41 that talk about how to hold the priesthood are for women AND men.

Remember, the priesthood is here to heal others. No priesthood ordinance is for yourself. You typically don't give yourself the sacrament or lay your hands on your own head to give a healing blessing. Every priesthood ordinance is always outwardly focused on others. Even ecclesiastical managing and judgeship must always be all about healing other humans.

In fact, there is no way to exercise the priesthood in any degree of selfishness. It's pretty clear right there in that same section of scripture: "The heavens withdraw themselves; the Spirit of the Lord is grieved; and when it is withdrawn, Amen to the priesthood or the authority of that man [or woman]" (Doctrine and Covenants 121:37). You can't have it. It's gone. You can only hold the priesthood as a healing force.

To hold this healing power, we need to seek four qualities, according to Doctrine and Covenants 121:41. And what are these four

---

3 See the "Priesthood" entry in Gospel Topics: churchofjesuschrist.org/study /manual/gospel-topics/priesthood.

qualities, these four power words? Gentle persuasion (meaning any persuasion I do in this healing effort needs to be gentle, never with a big stick), long-suffering (patience), meekness (meaning that I seek that higher power in how I behave and how I think), and love unfeigned (genuine, sincere, nontransactional love). These four words are the power words of Christ's gospel.

In my lifetime, I've had so many challenging moments that took me to my knees. They just pushed me to the wall and took the breath out of me. And every time that happened to me, I had this sense of inspiration. A little sentence came into my mind: **live your religion.** That was the answer to my seeking in the depths of my soul. When I asked the big questions in hard times, God just said, live your religion—not the checklist of commandments, but these basic, fundamental principles, these truths. Facing whatever challenge I had in front of me, I started to lay these four qualities on top of the situation, no matter what it was. I started to try to act in a way that was more long-suffering, with gentle persuasion, meekness, and love unfeigned.

That itself wasn't the answer. What happened was this: in doing those things and living those power words of the priesthood of healing, the answers came. By acting with those qualities, I got the answers that I sought.

When I faced a mountain of challenges and finally the answer came in prayer, "Live your religion," I thought, that's how you do it. Live your religion. The answer came as these same four qualities: lay long-suffering over this situation, lay meekness over the situation, lay gentle persuasion over the situation, lay love unfeigned over the situation. If I were going to *be* gentle persuasion, if I were going to *be* long-suffering, how would I act in this situation? As I did those things, I found myself leaving a transactional mindset and moving toward a nontransactional mindset. As I really focused on the other person in the relationship, the other part of the conflict, suddenly ideas came into my mind about what to do. It was as if the gate opened to more enlightenment. It's like God had answers for me—specific, actionable answers—but until I got my own selfishness out of the way, until I got to this place of love for others, God couldn't work with me.

These are all pieces of the puzzle about the vitality of the law of love, because all of this starts to combine together. Once you see this, almost every word from Christ—every parable, every lesson, every-thing—has this ennobling piece to it: the law of love.

8

THE LAW OF LOVE
IN FOOTBALL

When I thought about those four qualities (long-suffering, gentle persuasion, meekness, and love unfeigned), I didn't take them only as gospel concepts in a church setting. I knew that if it doesn't work in the huddle, it doesn't work.

Meekness? That wasn't going to get the ball across the goal line. Long-suffering? Nope. Gentle persuasion? Definitely not going to get it across the goal line. Love unfeigned? Probably not. But even in football, those four power words of the gospel helped me. I knew intuitively that a football player would respond just as any other human being. If they were seen more deeply and appreciated, they would be more likely to give it their all.

As a quarterback, the accountability rests with me, but when I really see my teammates deeply at key moments and appreciate their efforts, what happens is they see my accountability and they immediately become even more accountable themselves. If I see you as my partner, if my success is your success, then you match my 100% effort with your own.

Because I do Monday night football as a sports commentator, I get around a lot to see the teams. I'll watch a team warm up and see them interact, and the most successful teams just act differently. I can see that they have those rooted qualities of selflessness. That's why they're good. It doesn't matter what play they call or what defense they run. You can see that connectivity between the members of the team, which just continues to build as they go through these shared experiences together. They sacrifice for each other and they're willing to go further for each other and deal with more trauma and face more challenges together. Under those relationships is selflessness, really seeking the success of the people around them.

REGGIE WHITE, "MINISTER OF DEFENSE"

Here's another example. Reggie White was six foot six, maybe six foot seven, 375 pounds. Don't believe the stats you read online about him weighing 300 pounds. That's just aspirational. He was the biggest human I've ever met, but he was big in a perfectly proportioned way—just a larger, perfect athlete. He was stronger than everyone, faster than everyone. And he was a fierce competitor. Reggie played for the Philadelphia Eagles, then he played for the Green Bay Packers for years. I faced Reggie in some of the biggest games in my life.

Every time I ever played him, I knew that Reggie was going to be such a pain. No one could block him. He just threw people out of the way. And you could hear him. When he competed, he competed loudly, full throttle. You could hear him screaming and hollering, and it was always like, *here comes Reggie, let me get rid of the ball.* A lot of times I didn't. He was paid millions of dollars to get to me. Quarterback is going down—Reggie was going to make sure of it.

But personally, we were fast friends. Reggie and I went back a ways. He knew my dad. Reggie and I developed this tremendous friendship. We met at the Hula Bowl All-Star game, back in our college days. We came out as rookies together in 1984; he went to the USFL (United States Football League) like I did, playing with the Memphis Showboats. He was a Christian man, a man of God, an ordained Baptist minister. They called him "the Minister of Defense."

I went to pro bowls with Reggie, and before or after a game he would invite the players to come to a chapel. He would preach and challenge them to be baptized. I went to his services and found them very enjoyable and incredibly uplifting. Once in Hawaii, I went back to the hotel after Reggie preached. I looked out the window to see Reggie baptizing these other pro bowl teammates in the ocean off the shore. He was just an energetic pastor of good will. He was a seeker. God was a quest for him, not a place of respite but a place of effort—unnerving effort.

But on the field, when Reggie was charging forward with every ounce of his being, this huge human trying to get to me, to earn the sack—the second he got me, I was his friend. He would grab me, then turn and let me fall down on top of him so I wouldn't get hurt. And then he would want to talk, panting, totally out of breath, saying, "Steve, how are you doing? Haven't talked to you for a long time. How's it going? How's your folks?"

I thought to myself, *How do you think it's going? I just got sacked!*

I would say, "Reggie. Not so good, bro. Not so good right now. But my folks are fine, thanks for asking. Let's talk later, OK?"

A few plays later I heard him. Here he came again, charging like a bull, yelling at the top of his massive lungs. He tackled me and turned again so I could land on him as I went down, and said, "So anyway, where are you staying? Do you stay here off-season?"

I felt like half the time Reggie wanted to sack me just so he could talk to me. I had to convince him, "Reggie, I'll buy you dinner. Let's just talk after. I don't want to see you on the field anymore."

Reggie just amazed me. In that adrenaline-filled environment, the physical challenge, the intense emotional and mental effort of playing professional football in front of thousands and thousands of people, most human beings react to the environment. They become a part of that aggressive world around them; that's how they find success. Reggie could be part of that, with the same adrenaline, the same intensity and the same competitiveness, but then there was a flash of a change and he was your friend. He could find common ground.

Reggie lived the law of love. He didn't have to cushion my fall as he took me down or engage in friendly chatter with me, his opponent. But Reggie loved as God loves, expecting nothing in return.

I can compete and I can have friendship, two things that don't usually go together very well. But with effort, I can hold them both.

BEING SPIRITUALLY ATHLETIC

There are other combinations of things in our lives where we have to hold both. For example, we are asked to forgive even when we're offended. What did Christ say? You must forgive those who despitefully use you (see Matthew 5:44). Think about it—if you've ever been despitefully used, this is a hard standard. We are asked to do spiritually athletic things, difficult things. To be a Saint is to be spiritually athletic.

To be spiritually athletic means to take the qualities of being an athlete—tremendous effort, flexibility, commitment, motivation, teamwork, focus, control, discipline—and apply those same qualities as I seek to live the law of love. I've never pulled more muscles or twisted more knees than while trying to live those four power qualities: gentle persuasion, long-suffering, meekness, and love unfeigned. Trying to be a Saint in an entropic world means that everything about it is a challenge. Everything is corrupting and corroding all around you, including yourself. The rigor of it tests the spirit. You can't just sit on the couch and passively expect to master those four qualities while you change the channel. That quest is going to take every inch of yourself, all the discipline and effort you can muster. It's going to draw on all of your abilities and expose your weaknesses.

The greatest athletes in the world that I've seen are performing incredible feats despite gravity and challenges and opponents and weather and the rules of the game. Like those great athletes, we can be spiritually athletic as we harness our humanity through living the law of love, to propel us into eternity.

These places of Zion, these centropic or perpetual places—there is no exclusiveness about them. Zion is always open to all. There is no scarcity of salvation. There is room for everyone.

The scriptures talk about working out our own salvation. And that is true: we are responsible in the end. The accountability for my actions does rest with me. Only Christ knows where that account-ability starts and stops. Only He knows the unique DNA that we inherited, or abuses that we received, or the individual gifts God gave us. We can take it all in and alchemize it for ourselves, through Christ's healing power. Each person has to figure it out for them-selves, with God's help, and find the full measure of who they can be—the full measure of their creation. We should be careful to re-spect how complex and intimate that is, and honor others as they go through that same process. We can't judge another person's jour-ney—that's between them and God. It's not our journey, and we just can't know what God is up to in their lives. That journey is personal and private and singular.

Working out my salvation sounds like a transactional, individual thing. But remember that Elder Uchtdorf said, "Salvation cannot be bought with the currency of obedience" ("The Gift of Grace," *Ensign*, May 2015). I can't actually work it out myself, finding my salvation. I find it in losing myself. And that's exactly what Christ said. Lose yourself and you'll find yourself (see Matthew 10:39; 16:25). So working out your salvation is not a singular act.

In fact, Jesus said "lose yourself and you'll find yourself" not once but twice: once to the Twelve Apostles as He sent them off on missions (see Matthew 10:39) and again, six chapters later, to the larger crowd of disciples that followed Him (see Matthew 16:25). When Christ repeats an instruction, He means it.

Some people hear "lose yourself" and think they will lose their identity if they follow Christ. But becoming Christlike doesn't mean turning into plain vanilla. You still hold on to your one-of-a-kind personality, your character traits (even the quirky ones), and your unique preferences that make you who you are. You know who you are and you know what you know, including the fact that you're not fully developed. The law of love asks everything of you. You bring your whole self to the law of love, in a selfless way (that's the irony of it). Then God expands you into the infinite, into perpetuity.

When we're on the finishing track, our North Star is not ourselves, not even seeking our own salvation, but seeking the healing of others. It's our deepest desire, what we want more than anything—for others to be healed. Then we feel the gravitational pull toward covenant-keeping as we intuitively follow the Master Healer. Seeking the healing of Jesus's children ironically delivers the very exaltation that we can't seek for its own sake. It's a virtuous cycle that never ends.

In the same way, we can't truly achieve peace by selfishly seeking it. If we do, other people may just become impediments to our personal quest for peace. But if we truly desire the healing of others, then peace pours into our souls with the most astonishing rush of spiritual enlightenment and knowledge and perspective.

Living the law of love is not easy, but it is so worth it. That's why we have to be spiritually athletic.

THE ONLY WAY OUT IS TO GO THROUGH IT— I CAN'T GO AROUND

Speaking of being spiritually athletic, I'm the kind of guy that faces into challenges (most of the time). It's taken years of hard work going *through* things, but it's the only way out. I can't go around. I learned this the hard way.

I had severe separation anxiety when I was growing up. As a kid, I was fearless during the day, especially when I had a ball in my hand. I never missed a day of school from kindergarten through high school and scored straight A's. But at nighttime, I needed to be home.

People would say, "Hey, sleep over at Eddie's house."

I would always say, "No. I don't want to do that." I didn't know why. I would make up something so I didn't feel so weird, like, "I have practice," or "Gotta go to church." It wasn't until I was in my thirties that I learned that it's a genetic thing. Separation anxiety is sprinkled all throughout my mom's family, but I didn't know it at the time.

I had a terrible first semester at BYU. I didn't even unpack my bags. I literally lived out of my suitcase the whole semester. I told my roommate every day that I was going home. I made it to Christmas somehow. Through all the anxiety and throwing up in the bathroom and stomachaches and everything, I made it. I was used to somehow powering through pain, physical and emotional. Sometimes it was sheer brute force of will.

At Christmastime, I was home with my family, the one place that I felt safe. But after a while, I kind of wanted to go back to college. Suddenly I realized, *Oh my gosh, now I have two homes.* It was the most amazing feeling to think I was going to be okay. There were two places that I could feel safe. And who knows, maybe there might eventually be ten places that I felt safe, or maybe one day there would be thirty places I felt safe.

I played football for BYU. I was All-American and almost won the Heisman trophy. In my senior year they took me to the draft. The Bengals were going to draft me. And I thought to myself, *Oh my gosh, I don't know anyone in Cincinnati. I would never want to be there alone. I'll never make it.* The option to go to Los Angeles was a great thing because I knew people in Los Angeles and there are more Latter-day Saints, and I'd figure it out. People always wonder why I went to the USFL. It was because I knew people in LA, and I didn't know anyone in Cincinnati.

And so I agreed to the contract in LA. Then they wanted to announce it. There I was in college and it had finally become my safe place, and I had to go to LA to sign the contract. It had all been theoretical until this point. The owner's plane picked me up in Provo and flew me down to LA for this huge signing ceremony. Suddenly it hit me that I needed to move to Los Angeles and do this. Jim Hill was interviewing me (he's still a sportscaster in LA after all these years). I fainted, right there in the interview. I kind of lost my balance and started to fade because I was just completely overwhelmed. The table caught me, and I came back. Then it dawned on me. *Oh, no. How was I going to do this? Did I think that this would be all fun and games?*

I flew home alone to Salt Lake City with two massive checks in my pocket, the signing bonus and the first paycheck. There I was, just a college kid about to graduate, with $20 in my wallet, trying to make it from day to day. I didn't even have a credit card. And I was pocketing two checks worth $2.5 million. I thought to myself, *What am I going to do? What am I going to do?* I didn't want the burden that would come with being an instant millionaire, with all the expectations. The checks felt like a ball and chain. I remember thinking,

How can I throw these checks out of the plane? There was no window to open. I just wanted to throw them out.

Then it came to me: I would give all the money to the Church. I could just announce that I'm giving all the money to the Church and play for free, because that way I won't have that pressure. Then I'll figure out how to move down to LA and everything else, but I cannot play for this money and all these expectations and this worldwide fame.

I said to the pilot, "Excuse me, look, you've got to find someone from the Mormon Church, someone high up that I can go see right now. I need to give these checks to them." I had the pilot get on the radio and find someone that I could meet with as soon as I landed. That was how I was going to solve this anxiety. I was in a really bad spot. So the pilot got on the radio, and he came back and gave me a piece of paper. He had written Elder Neal A. Maxwell's address on the paper. Eventually we landed and all the media was there. I kind of talked my way through that. Then I got in my car and drove right to where Elder Maxwell lived.[1]

I knocked on sweet Elder Maxwell's door around 8:30 p.m. He said, "Brother Young, so nice of you to come by. Come on in." I told him everything that was going on and handed the checks to him. I was going on the *Good Morning America* show on TV in the morning, and I would announce that I was giving all the money to the Church.

Elder Maxwell said, "Steve, honestly, your heart is really great,

---

1 Elder Maxwell had asked to meet with me at his home once before. When I was playing college football at BYU and first started receiving national media attention, he wanted to make sure I was holding up under so much scrutiny.

but that's actually not the principle. The principle is that you have been given an opportunity to show how to behave in this situation, rather than avoid it. You need to go through it. Simply giving away the money in some ways might be avoiding the very experience that God intends for you to have. Sometimes the most rigorous experiences of this life should not be avoided." Then he handed back the checks. "These belong to you."

I couldn't say no to him, but my body was saying, *No, I'm giving you the money.* Elder Maxwell gave me a blessing, and afterward, he said, "Steve, you're going to be fine. You have great meekness. You're going to be fine." And I left thinking, *He did not help me at all. He just ruined my day. Why didn't he just take the money and let me move on?* I was desperate in a way that only people with severe separation anxiety can feel. I wanted to go around the challenge, but deep down I knew I had to go through it.

Elder Maxwell's point was this: you need to find God's hand in this situation. It is going to be a hard path, but you're going to have to find God's hand in it. And we'll all be with you. Whenever I go see the General Authorities, they always say, you know, Steve, you're great. We love you. Good luck. Good luck out there. Which is really the right way to do it.

In giving me that blessing, Elder Maxwell gave me the ability to live this out. Probably donating money to the Church wouldn't have solved the core issue. He probably recognized this would just kick the core issue down the road. It wouldn't solve anything. There would still be all these expectations of me; it didn't matter to the team where I put the money. I had to go through it. So Elder Maxwell rejected my donation. And I did move to LA and I did play football and somehow I survived.

Today, the crushing anxiety, the shortness of breath, the stomachaches, the constant worry—those are all in the rearview mirror. My life is completely different. That level of anxiety, I just don't feel it. Sure, life isn't always simple. But I don't give up. Ever. When I'm lost and I don't know what to do, I remember that I can't go around. I just have to go through. That's part of being spiritually athletic.

TRYING TO BE SOMEONE ELSE

When I was recruited to play for the 49ers, I was hired to replace their star quarterback, Joe Montana. He had just had his second back surgery that was expected to end his career. But when I arrived in San Francisco, Joe was recovering and was back in the game. That left me as Joe's backup for four years. Four long years.

My first instinct was that I wanted to copy Joe Montana, because he was the best quarterback in the game. But I realized quickly that copying him was not going to work, because we did things differently. I was very focused on trying to win the quarterback position, but over time I realized he had already established himself and was so far ahead. He had already won two Super Bowls and was the king. Winning that position was going to be one of the biggest challenges of my life.

As I raced around trying to do that, the law of diminishing returns kicked in. The harder I tried, the more focused I got, and the more intense I was.

And I mean intense. There was no time off. I was single at the time, and I was laser focused on doing this. That's all I cared about, all I could think about.

In many ways, it was like David and Goliath. I was David, of course, Joe was Goliath, and I didn't have any rocks. I did my best, but I hated being the backup. It wasn't personal between us, but it was like a cold war.

I give Joe a ton of credit. Despite all the angst around it, he and I never had a cross word. We played lots of golf together. Despite the awkwardness, throughout the time we were on the 49ers, I really supported him and he supported me. Whenever he was on the field, I tried to give him everything that I had to make sure that we won. When I was playing, I tried to prepare myself the best I possibly could. We have tremendous respect for each other's abilities. I saw Joe do things on the field that to this day I've never seen any other human being do.

During those four years while I was his backup, Joe Montana led the team to two Super Bowls and was twice named MVP. And I had to watch. That was my most hated thing in the world—to watch. I wanted to play. Then in 1991, Joe got hurt and was going to be out the entire season. So it was my year, my time. I knew that there were going to be comparisons. I knew that I had inherited that part of my life. But I had no idea how insane it would get when I started to play regularly.

Every game was dissected through the perspective of how it would have been different if Joe had played. Throughout 1991, the first eight games or so, we were not great. We had just won the Super Bowl twice. We were supposed to be great. Why aren't we great?

Well, that's pretty easy. Steve's here, right? Every game, every play, every word was compared. It became so maddening. I noticed over the weeks it started to wear on me.

I would get in the car and tune the radio to the easy listening station. Barry Manilow would quit singing and then suddenly the announcer would come on and say, "Well, Steve Young is not Joe Montana."

Or I would be in the grocery store. The clerk was checking out the person in front of me and inevitably that conversation went like this: "Well, how about Steve Young, he's no Joe Montana." You think I'm joking, but it was everywhere. I sank into a depression in this effort to try to replace him. I thought, *Well, that is not working*. I went into a hole of anxiety.

Fear and anxieties are kind of innate to me. As I mentioned, when I was little, I didn't leave home very often. Even going to college was a death-defying experience. But this was a whole new level of fear and anxiety.

There were nights when I would go to bed, and I would just be glad that the day was over. The next morning at the first crack of light, my body just woke up and I had that dread and the sense that I just couldn't do it another day and wondered how I was going to get up and go to work. I would just lie there for a while with that sick stomach feeling. This went on for weeks and months.

Then the dread became resentment. I resented the rest of the team because they certainly weren't as focused as I was on trying to help me achieve our goal. They clearly were underinvested and I was overinvested, and I would grumble, *This is lousy, this is not fair, the people are not treating me right, the media isn't looking at this the right way, the beat writers are writing stories that aren't even true, they don't have the right context . . .* The whole thing had kind of collapsed on me as I was trying to achieve this great thing.

So we went to play the Los Angeles Raiders in the LA Coliseum and we got beat 12–6 in front of 90,000 fans. I spoke earlier about that terrible game. The last play of the game we had a chance to win it. I was scrambling around, and Jerry Rice was open in the end zone (I learned this later watching the film). I was overwrought, I was desperate, and I just didn't see him. I got sacked and the game ended and everyone went into the locker room. It was kind of a low point when I could feel my own teammates thinking, *This is not working—where's Joe?* Everyone in my world, from the players I worked with, to the media, the newspapers, the radio, people at the grocery store: everywhere I went, it was just squeezing down on me.

That Tuesday was the NFL players' day off. So Monday night I flew back to Salt Lake, where I was home safe. I just needed to get away for a minute. I went to see my brother, who was at the University of Utah medical school. We just walked around downtown Salt Lake, with me basically lamenting all the things I just told you but with more emotion.

My brother gave me a reality check. He told me, "Steve, you're getting paid a million dollars. It would be my dream to play professional football. I've got three kids and I'm broke. I'm trying to survive in med school." I couldn't even hear his needs. I couldn't even listen to what he was going through. I thought, *I don't know how I'm going to make it to Christmas. I'm going to collapse.*

"DO YOU WANT TO SEE HOW GOOD YOU CAN GET?"

I got on the plane to go back to San Francisco and sat next to Stephen Covey, author of *The 7 Habits of Highly Effective People*. I had been around Stephen Covey and I knew his kids well, but I had never really had a chance to talk to him. He asked, "How are you doing?"

During the flight, for the next thirty or forty-five minutes, I just unloaded on him in great detail about how disastrous and terrible the situation was. I told him, "I wish I played tennis, I wish I played golf . . . all these expectations . . . Joe Montana . . . the 49ers . . ."

Stephen listened, which is one of his real talents. At the end he said, "Steve, that's a lot. I can feel where you are right now. Do you mind if I ask you a couple of questions?" I said sure.

Stephen said, "To begin with, fifty guys on a team, eleven on the field, is too many. It's been scientifically proven that seven is the maximum number of people that can work effectively together. Eleven is chaos. But when you're successful, there is magic in too many people achieving something together. That's where the magic is."

Stephen continued, "Your owner, Eddie DeBartolo—I've heard that he's quite an innovative owner."

"Oh my gosh, yes, he's the first owner who saw players as partners, and that's unheard of. We were chattel."

"Yeah, I heard that. I would really like to meet him one day. He seems like a really interesting man. What about Bill Walsh, your coach?"

"Oh my gosh, yes, Bill is so innovative in his offense and how he looks at the players holistically: their health, their mental health, their marriages, what they need . . ."

"Yeah, I heard that. I would really like to meet him one day. He seems like a really interesting guy. Joe Montana—he's still on the team, on the sidelines, right?"

"Well, that's the problem, that's the whole issue."

"But if you needed a mentor, could you talk to him and ask him questions?"

"Yeah, yeah, I could do that."

"Hmm . . . interesting." And then he looked at me. He said, "Steve, I travel the world looking for platforms—companies, families, organizations, governmental agencies—anywhere someone has built a platform that allows people iterative possibilities to see how good they can get. I look for those qualities that make that happen and I try to amplify those qualities. To me that's what life is about: iterative opportunities to see how good you could get."

He continued, "Listening to your story, I don't know of anyone that I've ever met, anywhere in the world, who is in a better place with a better platform to go see how good he can be."

I remember that feeling. My whole world just shifted. My life just changed right there. Talk about transfigured eyesight. I saw myself, my situation, and everyone around me in a completely different light. Stephen said to me, "This is difficult because not everyone wants this. But do you want to see how good you can get? Because in that quest, you might find out that you are not nearly as far along as you thought. But do you want to take the risk to find out how good you can get?"

I looked him right in the eye and I said, "Yes, I want that."

"Then you are one of the luckiest men I know."

I raced down to work the next day praying that I hadn't lost my job because of my attitude and my dismal performance and the blame game and the depression. It was the shift in perspective: the ability to see in a new way with a broader, deeper vision. It really changed my professional life, my career and my whole world view, when I saw achievement as a quest to see how good I could get.

The next year we played the Dallas Cowboys. They were the big dogs. It's a little unusual to do this, but I went racing over to Troy Aikman. Usually you just go over and shake hands and say "Have a good game" or whatever. But I said, "Troy, I'm so glad you're here! I'm on a quest to see how good I can get, and I can only find out against the best, and you guys are the best, and I'm so grateful you're here."

Troy said, "Yeah, thanks for coming too," looking at me like I was talking crazy.

That quest to find out how good I could get: I did find out. The next season I was NFL MVP. Something that had seemed miserable was actually an opportunity. It spun into something well beyond anything I could have ever imagined. And in the spirit of nontransactional relationships, I also wanted to be the healing agent that allowed others to see how good they could get, too. Could I free them up to go do that? Because I certainly didn't win football games alone. I could throw the ball all day long, but I needed Jerry Rice and Brent Jones to catch it. Every member of that team was doing their job. It's the law of love in football: in supporting others to see how good they can get, I also found out how good I could get, and together we achieved something monumental.

One of my favorite moments in my professional life was in the locker room after the Super Bowl. We always knelt and said the Lord's Prayer together at the end of every game. Afterwards, the jubilation was just incredible, we were all so euphoric at what we had accomplished together. I looked around and there was this feeling like, oh my gosh, WE DID IT. There was a connectivity that I will never, ever forget, that together all of us had done something super special. Looking at everyone's faces was just magic—seeing what we had just achieved as a team. Winning the Super Bowl was like staking a flag atop Mount Everest. We had finally reached the summit. And it had happened by our living the qualities of the law of love: patience, long-suffering, helping each other find out how good we could get.

This law of love stuff—I said to myself, you mean it's not just true on Sunday mornings in the chapel but also during Chargers vs. 49ers? This really works.

HUMILITY: MICKEY MOUSE'S BODYGUARD

The night before the Super Bowl, the public relations guy for the 49ers came to me and put a contract in front of my face. He said that if I signed it, and if I won the Most Valuable Player award in the game, that I would be the one that yelled into the camera at the end of the game.

They would say, "Now that you're the MVP of the Super Bowl, what are you going to do?"

And I would yell at the camera, "I'm going to Disneyland!"

My family and I are Disneyland fanatics. For me it was really exciting because it was like being on the Wheaties box. It was one of those things I had grown up seeing, something that all my heroes had done.

The next day, as it turned out, I did end up being MVP of the game. I was so excited that we had won the game and that the pressure was off. Honestly, I was more relieved than happy. All the years I played football my dad would say, "Just have fun," but I would always look at him puzzled, like, *Fun? This is too much pressure to have fun!* But after the Super Bowl, when we had won the game and I was MVP, the pressure was off, and I was just ecstatic.

Well, the public relations guy came to me and said, "Remember, we've got this deal that you're going to yell into the camera that you're going to Disneyland." So I did. I thought, *Wow, that's the neatest thing that I ever did, or ever even thought about doing.* It was like an out-of-body experience, like, *Oh my gosh, it's happening to me,* but it was like me watching myself do this. It was crazy.

Later that night during the celebration, the same PR guy came to me again. He said, "Oh, by the way, that wasn't a metaphor. I don't know if you read the contract, but you actually have to go to Disneyland. And you have to go tomorrow." Well, this was a surprise to me. I hadn't had the time the night before the game to read the contract.

So I flew back from Miami to San Francisco and then went to Anaheim. The next night, there I was in front of the castle at Disneyland on a huge float with gold and red streamers (the colors of the 49ers). On the side of the float it read, "Steve Young, Super Bowl MVP." On top were me and Mickey Mouse and the Disneyland band. Down Main Street we went.

Remember, I had just come off one of the most euphoric experiences of my life. All the pressure had been relieved and there were all these wonderful feelings and I was at Disneyland, which I love, with Mickey Mouse at my side. People just loved the Super Bowl and they were yelling, "Steve, you're the man!" "Steve, you're the greatest!" "You're the king!" "Joe who?"

I found myself lost in the moment and thought to myself, *I have made it. I've reached the top of the mountain and I never want to come down.*

I so relished that moment and wished the parade could have gone on forever. You may not know this, but Walt Disney built Main Street so that it's an optical illusion. It's much shorter than it looks. The parade lasted about six minutes, but it felt like thirty seconds. Very quickly the parade ended, the band turned to go backstage, and it was kind of quiet.

Then I noticed two little boys sitting on the curb dressed alike, as parents do, so that kids are easier to find. There they were in their red shirts and Levi's jeans, six and eight years old. The younger one looked up and saw Mickey Mouse. His jaw dropped. He started to walk toward the float, mesmerized. But before I could say anything or do anything in fear that he might get hurt, his brother grabbed him by the shirt and pulled him back, saying, "You can't get near him. The big guy won't let you." Meaning me.

Right there reality came flooding in as I looked at this eight-year-old. The euphoria was over. No matter how I felt about it, to this young boy I was Mickey Mouse's bodyguard.

I have reflected on that moment for years and years because of the impact that it had and how it affected me. I immediately realized that yes, I had made it to the top of Mount Everest, but six minutes later I had another role to play and another perception to deal with.

For me humility is sometimes forced, sometimes served cold. But I think it should be worn like our favorite pair of comfortable shoes, like our home base that we are always connected to. Sometimes humility is one of the most important pieces of my life. Whether I'm in the dregs of affliction or placing the flag on the top of Mount Everest, I need humility to find God's purpose in all those moments in my life, from the top to the bottom. Not worldly humility, like putting myself down or being servile, but Godly humility, like God is in control, not me, with a plan for me, and my deep desire is to follow it.

I'll always be grateful for those little kids who vividly reminded me that yes, you can put the flag on top, but twenty seconds later, you've got to climb down, and life goes on.

Humility and being vulnerable are some of the foundational principles of the law of love. Humility is meekness. It's a necessary precondition because it's essential to staying right-sized in relation to other people and to God. I can't overlay the law of love if I'm starting from a puffed-up place of self-importance, looking down on others or thinking I know better than God. It goes back to that clear voice I received: "Live your religion."

9

THE LAW OF LOVE
IN BUSINESS

At the age of thirty-eight, after playing eighteen professional seasons, I decided to retire. I thought, *Now I've got another half of my life I've got to go live.* My dad always told me you have to have a dream and a plan. The dream? Be the best football player. The plan? Finish college and go to law school. Then I started to play professional football and got paid a lot of money, and I told my dad, "The dream IS the plan! Now they are the same!"

He didn't miss a beat and said, "No, because the average NFL career is three years. What are you going to do after? What's the plan?" That is why I went to law school while I was playing in the NFL.

Besides, I was bored while I was backing up Joe Montana and had nothing to do. Studying my heart out in law school kept me occupied. I remember going directly from a Super Bowl parade one day to being in class the next day, getting hammered by my professor because I had missed the first few weeks of the semester.

While I was playing football, my 49ers teammates and I began investing with a few venture capital firms. We traded access to the locker room for opportunities to invest. One thing led to another, until that process led to my current career in a middle-market private equity firm.

Now my life routine and choices are not as predictable. Life as a professional football player is challenging and all-encompassing, but it's cloistered behind the NFL walls. Finishing law school, getting married, starting my family, starting my career, being out in the world, I've faced some amazing challenges during which I thought to myself, *How am I going to do this? How do I attack this? How do I even start accomplishing it?* It was a really challenging, emotional time.

After many struggles in prayer, the same answer came: Live your religion. Lay on those same qualities of gentle persuasion, long-suffering, meekness, and love unfeigned. I tried to practice this even in business settings.

You wouldn't think that the professional sports world and the high-stakes world of private equity would be natural springboards into the law of love. But it works everywhere.

Private equity is like the NFL in some ways. It's a highly competitive, tip-of-the-spear kind of place. The people that are successful in this field are really achievement-oriented in their relationships. But for me, the real question is, how do you make people feel? Sometimes the smartest people understand the science of finance, but they don't understand human beings. Everyone can benefit from leaning into their ability to understand the human capacity. It really does build lasting success when you develop the softer skills of relationship-building and awareness of others.

My job now is negotiating big acquisitions for our firm. It's always a multi-dimensional conversation with great complexity. But I've learned to see it from a 360-degree perspective.

In private equity negotiations involving billion-dollar transactions, having it out in the boardroom amongst ourselves tends to be a zero-sum kind of experience. I thought to myself, *Of all the odd places to try this law of love. But what if I did it in one of these heated negotiations?* I decided to try it. It was amazing how someone on the other side often responded. In a way, you are vulnerable and can be taken advantage of, but taking that position can also attract those folks who are willing to collaborate. I've found that most people will tend to seek common ground if given the opportunity. The more I did it, the more success I had. All of a sudden, I wasn't looking for the last dollar.

Business is, by its very nature, transactional. And if I leave it there, many times it ends up in the usual zero-sum exit ramps. The enlarging and ennobling effort to overlay the law of love even in this environment has been a surprising enterprise.

Every business relationship can be heavily influenced by non-transactional behaviors. Although there are usually contracts that underlie most relationships, my experience is that most of the time those contracts are rarely used to decide how to manage, govern, and problem-solve.

Taking an abundant stance starts with the fundamental belief that there is a middle ground. Even if there is no middle ground, I can at least approach the situation without the self-focused aim to get everything I can get. In the end, an abundant approach to business is not a science but an art, like all relationships: seeing others deeply, with an empathetic view.

That attitude is a gravitational pull that draws people into it when exposed to it. There is a naturalness to it. Even in a business context, I try to never be drawn into a zero-sum game. With almost everyone that I run into in my work, when I engage them in this way, immediately a different spirit comes into the negotiation. Even when things are going poorly or things turn south, because we've built on a foundation of abundance, that spirit helps us go through hard things. We can still be collegial and cordial when both people want to hold on to that spirit of abundance. It's a beautiful thing. Even the handshakes at the end are different. That old saying is really true: no one remembers what you say, but they remember how you made them feel.

It may seem that this softer approach will come off as weak or put me at a disadvantage. My experience is that fighting with knives out only leaves a bloody trail. If you are focused on the last dollar, then it's difficult to take an abundant approach. The more intense the environment (both in business and in football), the more profound the impact of the law of love. In fact, it's our only hope in these intense environments.

That's why the law of love is undefeated. And that's not just in religion. The law of love is undefeated in all of humanity: in football and business and personal relationships. Whether you're an atheist or a humanist or something else, the law of love is undefeated, and its author is Christ, even if someone doesn't know Him or hasn't even thought about who He is. The law of love is not limited to covenant-keepers. That's why I know it's true: because it's not just true in certain places or certain circumstances or under certain conditions. There are no qualifiers for the law of love. It is undefeated everywhere.

MAYHEM IN THE BOARDROOM

I warned you that I'm no expert in the law of love; I'm in process too. I've got blood on my own hands here. Early on, before I understood much about these principles, I had an experience with a business owner I'll call Michael.[1] My private equity firm bought the business from him, and we had some very difficult conversations around control, essentially. I had taken the perspective that only one person can be in control. If there wasn't a quarterback, things would devolve—and the quarterback needed to be the new CEO we hired. After we bought his business, Michael agreed that he would take a role as the chairman of the board and wouldn't be involved in the day-to-day operations anymore.

But Michael kept hanging around the business. Finally the new CEO called me and said, "Hey, this guy is driving me crazy." I had to call Michael and ask him to back off and give the new management some breathing room.

Michael answered, "Well, what do you want me to do? I can't even walk around?"

---

1 Name has been changed.

I said, "Look, in the end, it's about people giving people space. You're so dynamic and such a strong person and . . ."

Michael said, "Okay, okay."

Then about a month later, the CEO called me and said, "Look, it's either him or me."

I said, "Michael, we've got to meet. Let's get together." We met in the boardroom, without the CEO. I went into it thinking, the CEO said he can't work with this guy, and because the CEO didn't see any place for Michael to contribute, I didn't see a place for Michael to contribute either. I looked at it as a zero-sum game.

So I said, "Michael, you've got to go." And that created an argument. I have had very few arguments in my life, but this was an argument that escalated to the point where Michael picked up a chair and threw it at me. He wasn't necessarily aiming for me, and he didn't mean to hurt me, but he threw the chair in frustration and anger.

All it was, in the end, was an inability to see each other's point of view. It didn't have to be a zero-sum game; there was a place to work through this very easily. I saw only winners and losers. The winner was the CEO, so the loser had to be Michael, right? I saw no other way around it. I didn't have the four power words to lay onto the situation: gentleness, meekness, long-suffering, love unfeigned.

But I knew that throwing a chair wasn't where I wanted the conversation to end. Our argument could have stopped the conversation at a standoff right there. Or I could have chosen to escalate it further. But I wanted to find common ground—I think we both wanted that. I knew we just had to keep talking until we found that common ground.

Once it got dramatic, I realized it was time to slow down and get to the root of it, to find out what was really wrong here. When the chair went flying, I was initially startled. But then my reaction was almost cheery: "Really? That's all you've got?" Michael took a deep breath and cracked the slightest grin (a little embarrassed, but still plenty frustrated). We looked at each other. Then I said, "Okay, now what are we going to do? Let's try to figure out what is driving this."

And so we continued the conversation. I listened. Michael talked. Eventually he said, "Having this back-and-forth discussion with you, I just now realize that I either need to run the business, or I need to leave the business. It's how I am; it's who I am. I can't be the chairman. I have to be in the business all the way, or I have to be out of it." Continuing the conversation got Michael to a peaceful place where he could feel good about it. In the end he realized that being out of the business altogether was really the best place for him as well as for the business.

Even now, ten years later, Michael and I stay in close contact. He's traveling the world. He calls me from the four corners of the earth, sailing the oceans, sending me pictures of him holding his baby granddaughter. He often says, "Steve, letting go of the business was the best thing that ever happened to me. I'm so grateful." I tease him that he thinks he's now a tremendous golfer. His family is traveling together, and they're closer than ever.

I went about it wrong, but eventually we found that place of peace because we continued the conversation in patience. In other words, inadvertently I ended up being long-suffering, with gentle persuasion and meekness. Even love. Not the warm fuzzy kind of love, but respect, being willing to try to stand in his shoes to have some empathy. It took a chair flying before I woke up and asked myself, "How can I bring healing to this situation?" Even before I understood about the law of love, there were elements that I enacted unawares that helped find a good ending for everyone: the company, Michael, and the new CEO.

This is how the law of love works. It works in high-pressure senior executive situations, where the professional stakes don't get any higher. If the law of love can help resolve conflict at the senior CEO level with a new buyer coming in, then the same principles can apply to the whole organization as well as individual lives.

10

THE LAW OF LOVE
IN A CHURCH SETTING

The folks I've talked to about the law of love run the gamut of faith: believers, former believers, nonbelievers, atheists, agnostics, humanists, etc. Many people from different walks of life have told me that these principles really resonated with them on so many levels. The law of love is everywhere. It's universal. But for me, the law of love sprang from a Church context.

GOD'S UNIMAGINABLE, REVOLUTIONARY LOVE FOR US

The "live your religion" spirit drives the foundational doctrine that we are in this educative space to become like God. If we are here to learn how to be more like God, then certainly we need to love like God. Loving like God cannot be transactional in the end. It can be transactional in the beginning, but not in the end.

Mother and Father in Heaven exist in a perpetual, nontransactional space. Their love is a healing love, ever present, never ending. It is selfless. We were together as a human family before this life, as spirit children of our Heavenly Parents. Their love for us began before we were even born here.

There is nothing we can do to limit our Heavenly Parents' love for us. Their love for us is infinite. "God loves you and there's nothing you can do about it," said Catholic theologian David Mangan in his book by the same title (Ventura, CA: St. Anthony Messenger Press/Servant Books, 2008).

President Thomas S. Monson agreed. He explained it this way in a general women's meeting: "Your Heavenly Father loves you—each of you. That love never changes. It is not influenced by your appearance, by your possessions, or by the amount of money you have in your bank account. It is not changed by your talents and abilities. It is simply there. It is there for you when you are sad or happy, discouraged or hopeful. God's love is there for you whether or not you feel you deserve love. It is simply always there" ("We Never Walk Alone," *Ensign*, Nov. 2013).

The parable of the prodigal son (see Luke 15:11–32) teaches this concept through Jesus's unforgettable storytelling. Remember the younger son who asked for his share of his father's inheritance? He "wasted his substance with riotous living," and returned home, starving and shameful (v. 13). The father received the son not with a scolding, but with a feast. *Boston Globe* columnist and former Catholic priest James Carroll wrote, "Jesus, speaking out of the Jewish tradition, described his Father's love in the parable of the prodigal son, as dependent on nothing but itself. No sacrifice needed; no religion, even; not good behavior either. God loves because God loves, period" (*Jerusalem, Jerusalem, How the Ancient*

City Ignited Our Modern World [Boston/New York: Mariner Books/ Houghton Mifflin Harcourt, 2012], 308).

YOUR WORTH, YOUR PURPOSE

In that same vein, your worth to God is set. It cannot change. There is absolutely nothing you can do to change your value to God. You don't have to earn God's love every day. I taught this to a group of youth on Zoom and watched while a young woman's shoulders visibly relaxed. I noticed her exhale in relief. It's true—God loves us no matter what. I don't have to earn straight A's, I don't have to win every game, I don't have to lose fifteen pounds, I don't have to be like my brother . . . I am loved and I have value, just as I am.

As that young woman that I met on Zoom grows up, she may face harder challenges, but the truth is the same: God loves her no matter if she's in prison, divorced twice, addicted to drugs, or any of a myriad of challenges. God's love never goes away.

Truman Madsen corrected some of his BYU students who said, "I don't amount to much. I'm not really one of those good ones," or, "I think I'm just basically telestial material."

He said, "The truth is that the embryo within the worst of us is divine. The truth is that there is nothing you can do to really destroy that fact" ("The Highest in Us," BYU devotional address, March 3, 1974).

With my infinite worth assured, I can turn my attention to my purpose. Why am I here? What is God's plan for me? That's easy: my purpose in life is to find a place to heal. Elder Neal A. Maxwell explained it in this thrilling quote: "The same God that placed that star in a precise orbit millennia before it appeared over Bethlehem . . . has given at least equal attention to placement of each of us in precise human orbits so that we may, if we will, illuminate the landscape of our individual lives, so that our light may not only lead others but warm them as well" (*That My Family Should Partake* [Salt Lake City: Deseret Book, 1974], 86).

That means that God has you exactly where God wants you. There are certain people that are placed in your life right now for you to heal. Your job each day is to ask God whom you need to help, who needs healing, and then go do it. Not to fix them, but to heal them. There is a difference: fixing is subjective, according to what I think needs fixing. Healing is God removing the pain of their wound. What heals them is their relationship with heaven. You are the conduit and partner with God to get that done. The best way I know how to think about this is to bring a spirit of healing (love, kindness, understanding, peace, patience, a listening ear) to every interaction we have, in every relationship we have. From the most intimate relationships in our families all the way to the guy that cuts us off on the road, whether that connection lasts for a brief moment or for a lifetime, we have the chance to bring a healing spirit to the relationship. Healing others must be our North Star—that ultimate goal we seek, despite our meanderings here or there—always looking to true north.

THE LAW OF LOVE IN OUR CONGREGATIONS

What if we did this in our congregations? What if we sat with people from different cultures, different marital status, different testimony status, different sexual orientation—and really tried to become the body of Christ? Jesus did that. He was just *with* everyone.

The congregation is a prime place to practice the law of love. Not just to go to church seeking a sense of righteousness for myself, but seeking to follow the higher law: I go to church to see others. To *really see* others. The smallest of things that I can do for others to make them feel better, to feel forgiven, to feel enriched, to be seen and understood, to feel heard because I listened to their stories and their backgrounds of why and how they had gotten here: all of that is where our congregations can find their highest calling. It's practice for transfigured eyesight. Even the smallest thing—smiling back at others as you pass—can help them feel better.

Our congregations are the place to practice. If every congregation with, say, 350 people, were all in a perpetual state of seeking transfigured eyesight, we could tap into such Christlike power. That's what Christ is talking about when He describes eternity and eternal life and perpetuity. He was talking science: the science Jesus held in His hands because of His Heavenly Parents.

Christ is saying, *I want you to seek the person that is the furthest from you, the person that is most unlike you. I want you to see that person more deeply.*

If you go as far as you can, it's actually unnerving. If you are seeking to abandon a transactional mindset, obedience isn't the North Star out in front of you. You thought you were heading for that goal of obedience, but that was just the preparatory law. Now you're lifting your gaze from obedience, and you've got your sights set straight on the celestial, bringing others with you, out of nothing more than pure love.

ONLY TWO MENTIONS: "THE ROYAL LAW OF LOVE"

Even though the law of love is so simple and seems so clear to me, I have not heard it spoken very often at all. I searched for it in the Church's Gospel Library and found only two conference talks, one in April 1978 by President Marion G. Romney, and one in October 1988 by Elder Marion D. Hanks of the Presidency of the Seventy, both titled "The Royal Law of Love." When I read those talks, I thought, *yes, that's it.* Elder Hanks said:

> Religion is not a thing apart from life. It is not principles and ordinances or missionary work or leadership as an end in themselves.
>
> It is a continuing marvel to me how well and with what grace and unselfish goodness so many live this sacred commandment [what he calls the royal law of love]. And it is sad to think that some may, **in a joyless version of 'the gospel,' miss the special blessings** awaiting on the path leading to the *highest* **joy through Christian service and sacrifice.**
>
> God and Christ love us with a mature, perfect love. The plan by which They lead requires mortal instruments of Their love. We have the great honor to be invited to be such instruments. **In this service we find the roots of most of those blessings that God wants us to enjoy.** The royal **law of love** is of sacred significance in the Lord's

program for his people. It is inseparable from Them and the spirit of Them. ("The Royal Law of Love," *Ensign*, Nov. 1988; emphasis added, capitalization modernized)

It was good to find those references, showing that someone was thinking about this decades ago. This law of love that is so vital and life-changing to me was actually specifically taught by President Romney and Elder Hanks all the way back in 1978 and 1988.

MINISTERING AND THE HIGHER LAW OF LOVE[1]

Then, in the April 2018 general conference, President Nelson and Elder Jeffrey R. Holland described a new work that the Church was going to do: a higher, holier work called ministering. As soon as I heard those words I was so energized to finally hear this being discussed over the pulpit.

Elder Holland said, "I warn you, a new name, new flexibility, and fewer reports won't make an ounce of difference in our service unless we see this as an invitation to care for one another in a bold, new, holier way, as President Nelson has just said. As we lift our spiritual eyes toward living **the law of love** more universally, we pay tribute to the generations who have served that way for years. I hope that legions more will grasp the Lord's commandment to 'be with and strengthen' our brothers and sisters (Doctrine and Covenants 20:53)" ("Be With and Strengthen Them," *Ensign*, May 2018; emphasis added).

I just fell over, like, *What did you say, Elder Holland?* I had been

---

1 See also page 25.

on this quest to understand the law of love, going through many, many experiences to recognize it. I believe Elder Holland understood intuitively that we can't do home/visiting teaching for credit; we have to do it in a selfless way. As Church members, we heard this whole thing about ministering, and what is different now? If our answer is "I just don't have to report it," then we've missed the most important piece. The emphasis in ministering is now on loving and healing the family, not making a visit and reporting it. Ministering can be either selfless or transactional. This subtle but vital change means we still go visit people, but it's widely different. It's our intent. It's the direction the ship leaves the port. Our intent is to heal, not file a report. Healing is what we seek. Through the law of love, we prepare our spirits to be ready to receive the inspiration to serve others and to bring Christ's healing power.

And it's not just our ministering families. Ministering is a practice. We're assigned a couple of people to go practice the law of love with as we interact in their lives, so that we can start to understand what that really means. Then we take that same spirit of healing and expand it outwards into all our relationships. What God really wants us to do is to bring the law of love with us in every relationship, every engagement, every interaction.

"NO MATTER WHAT, NO MATTER WHERE": MISSIONARIES AND EVERYONE

Recently I was asked to speak to some missionaries in our stake that had come home because of COVID. The leaders wanted me to fire them up and keep them going because they were home and they were supposed to be on their missions. Some were so depressed because they were stuck at home and not out there doing the work.

My immediate thought was to lay the law of love on that situation. I said to them: "Are you breathing? Do you have a pulse? Do you have any relationships at all in your life right now? It doesn't matter whether you're at home or in Madagascar or Bogotá, Colombia, or Tuscaloosa, Alabama—it doesn't matter. The call is to be a healer in every relationship that you're in, whether you're at home or in the field. In every relationship, if you just start seeking to heal others, that's the missionary effort in the end. Missionaries or I or anyone else do not save; only Christ saves. All we can do is provide space—healing space—for Christ and His Atonement, space for common ground, space for abundance."

When I finished speaking, one of the sweet sister missionaries said, "Brother Young, I'm really grateful for what you just said." She talked about a couple of experiences that really just hit me right square in the heart—just how much she naturally saw this law of love as the way forward. And she described it in such a beautiful way because she lived it. She was a natural healer, instinctively living these principles.

Right when she finished, another missionary stood. I happen to know him very well and he's just a wonderful human being. He said, "Brother Young, as you know, I am a can-do guy. There is nothing that I won't sacrifice when asked. I love doing whatever I'm asked to do. I just do it because I find such great goodness and grace in it. But what you're describing is very uncomfortable for me. It's something that I can't just go and do."

And I turned around and said, "Yeah, I know. I'm uncomfortable too. Trust me. This is not a place of comfort when God is asking you to do higher, holier things."

I think what this young elder was saying is that he loves the righteousness merit badge, like, "If I do what you're describing, I can't get the merit badge." And isn't that the point? The seeking of healing for others, in a nontransactional way, is the only way to achieve righteousness myself.

I thought it was very poignant that he was unnerved by it, and I can see why. I think we all are. As human beings, we love righteousness. We seek it. We want to know that we're righteous. We want to know that we're doing good. How many times in my life have I sought counsel so that someone would just tell me what to do? Point me in the right direction and I'll go there, full steam ahead. But when someone just asks you to love without transaction or reward, well, it's tough to wrap your head around it.

Even missionary work itself can be done in a nontransactional way. Some act as if my job is to teach you, and then your job is to be baptized or come back to church or whatever. It's a transaction. But what if you saw your goal not as baptism or reactivation, but loving that person on their journey, expecting nothing in return? Not baptisms to add to your list of converts, not a good report for the bishop or the mission president or anyone else. In fact, in some areas, missionaries no longer call the people they teach "investigators." They call them just "friends." Think of the power of that, both for the missionary or member and for their new friend.

Once a woman was meeting weekly with the missionaries for

over a year. She enjoyed the discussions and faithfully read the suggested scripture passages nearly every week, but she expressed no interest in baptism. When the missionaries were asked whether meeting with her was still worth their time, one said, "Our job as missionaries is to invite people to come unto Christ. If she's feeling closer to Christ, then our work is a success, regardless of whether she is ever baptized." That is admirable, inspiring, nontransactional missionary work.

If Christ were here today, I think He would have me sit down immediately and listen instead of talk. And then I think He would say, what have you been doing for 2,000 years? I've been trying to tell you about this law of love. I told you, it's the highest law. It's this nontransactional love that you must live because you can't earn the things you seek. You can't buy what you want in life because for those things, there is no money. No matter how many mountains you climb, Steve Young, how many trophies you earn, no matter what, none of that is what gets you home. Those conquered mountains and trophies will not bring the healing, the perpetual peace that you seek. It can never be elite or elect or based in a sense of self. Those things can be a start, a foundation, but it has to become a beautiful invitation that is bought without transaction, without a sense of ownership, without a sense of other. It can only be bought with a sense of healing and peace, leading to that place of perpetuity.

The goal is to come to Jesus Christ, follow Him, read about Him, act like Him, serve like Him—then share that feeling with others in a nontransactional, healing way.

"I'VE GOT YOUR BACK"

I mentioned earlier that when I joined the 49ers, I was hired to replace Joe Montana after an injury, except that he recovered and there we both were. My presence was irritating and Joe didn't like it, and all the other players knew he didn't like it, and he was "the king." Everyone fell in behind Joe and made me feel very uncomfortable and awkward, very "othered."

At one point while we were doing drills in practice, I did something wrong and someone laughed and said, "This guy's a joke," right in front of the others.

One of the defensive players, Ronnie Lott,[2] turned to the other guys and said, "Let me tell you something. My dad once told me when I was a kid that no matter where I went, no matter what happened, he had my back. And that's always mattered to me. I think it's super important at this moment that I tell you the same thing. Steve, come over here." I had no idea what to expect. He stood beside me, looked at the other players and continued, "Steve, I want you to know that I have your back, and I'm not going to put up with anyone that disrespects you. We're all in this together."

Ronnie had given me this gift of healing. He saw me, and he wanted to make sure that I was not feeling like an opponent inside my own team. It was such a gift to me. Certainly, his words impacted those around me, who treated me differently after that. But the biggest healing impact was for me, in the way I felt on my own home team. That impact reverberated for a long time.

---

2 I mentioned in Chapter 1 that Ronnie helped calm down Charles Haley during one of his tirades.

Ronnie was right. That same lesson applies to life. If we pull together, we're going further as a team of the human family. I'm not going to allow anyone to be othered while I'm around. We can challenge each other to be better, but we can do it with respect. No one has special elite status. We are in this together.

FELLOW SOLDIERS OF FAITH

Every human being was a part of the human family before this life, as spirits. That's an incredible thing to know: as I run into somebody on the street, no matter where I am anywhere in the world, no matter what their experiences, whether aborigines in Australia or businessmen in Finland, they all made a fundamental choice of faith to come to this earth, this place of opposition, and take a body. That redefines people to me, to know that they're born in faith, that they have already made that most fateful, faithful decision to choose to come to this earth. That premortal decision, that leap of faith, defines them more in the eternities than what is happening right in this second, or even a lifetime of choices. We're all fellow soldiers of faith, called to heal other fellow soldiers, on our way to immortality, just as C. S. Lewis said (see page 61).

In that knowledge of our fellow sojourners, the law of love starts to show us that we can't be a Church that seeks to be separate. We're a Church of a priesthood of healing, and not just for ourselves. All these fellow humans are rooted in faith, despite whatever they're doing. It doesn't matter. They're rooted in faith because they are here on this earth and made the right choice in that first world of spirits. What can I do to heal them? What relationship can I have with them? What can I change in how I behave? Then I'm like Johnny Appleseed with a sack of healing seeds, just throwing them out there every day.

OVER-ELEVATING OBEDIENCE VS. LAW OF LOVE

The second we become focused on obedience and over-elevate it, that's when it starts to devolve. Many people feel that the law of obedience is the highest law in heaven. I'm here to testify that if we over-elevate obedience, we are headed down a very, very challenging road because we've over-promoted something that needs to be properly understood.

Overloading obedience inside of our Church has brought us this othering, like we're special and we're better. That's the nature of self-interest in that kind of obedience.

I heard it said recently that the Church is wonderful from age zero to eighteen because we're teaching these preparatory, foundational principles through transactional, merit-badge theology. Then the rest of our life, we're just supposed to endure to the end. But really, that's the time to come over to the finishing track and explore this law of love.

That finishing track, the law of love, is never ending. It's so expansive. You'll receive so much more than you ever thought. But the only way to receive it is by not seeking it. If I'm obedient and it doesn't propel me forward into seeking others' healing as an adult, then I'm doing obedience wrong. The law of love doesn't steal from obedience; it changes its focus. In my small efforts experimenting on the law of love and trying to live it, I've noticed that the law of love has a natural gravitational pull to all of the laws and everything that is good. Here's how Elder Bruce C. Hafen described it in a BYU devotional:

> The first sacrifice (baptism) was about breaking out of Satan's orbit. The second one (temple endowment) is about breaking fully into Christ's orbit, pulled by His gravitational power, . . . consecrating ourselves spiritually, holding back nothing. As we feel the power of Christ's love pulling us toward Him, we anticipate the joy of His promise: "Be faithful and diligent . . . , and I will encircle thee in the arms of my love" (D&C 6:20). ("A Disciple's Journey," BYU devotional address, February 5, 2008)

That gravitational pull to the law of love is an indescribable experience. The ennobling, enriching wonder of the law of love and the scriptures and the experiences of Christ and His teachings and parables leads to a changed heart, a changed nature.

It really resonated with me that when we try to force obedience, the law of love is damned in compulsion. We can't be compelled to love. We can't be compelled to more Christlike thinking and behavior. God never forces us to do anything. He only invites and encourages.

Some fear that if we don't hammer the law of obedience, we will lose our grip on it and people will be less obedient. I remember teaching some of these concepts early on when I was just trying to figure it out. An elderly woman in the front row said, "Brother Young, I'm very uncomfortable with what you're talking about. You just want people to love, and what is this, like 1960s hippie stuff? This isn't going to work. I've tried to be obedient all my life. I just want to have the list and do my list. There is something beyond the list? What you're asking of me is not what I want to do."

I understood where she was coming from, and I respect her position, but I was frustrated because my words and my preparation were not enough to be ready to try to explain it. I wanted to honor her lifetime of obedience while simultaneously inviting her to a place beyond her checklist.

For me, when I practice the law of love, I do better with my relationship with God and commandment-keeping. But it doesn't happen overnight. It is an iterative, selfless spiritual practice that takes time. I can head in a selfless direction, only to veer back for some transaction or reward from another person or even God. I need to constantly refocus my effort in "losing myself." There is a discipline to it.

Think about something as wonderful as going to the temple. It's one of the highest things that you can be asked to do. You can go to the temple for credit. You can go to the temple to be seen by others, or so that you can tell the bishop or your spouse or set an example for your children. You can even go to the temple because you want to feel righteous, or you want to be in that place of peace. Those reasons to go to the temple—mostly good reasons—are still transactional. I'm going because I want to get something, like making a deal: I show up at the temple, and God will give me peace, or that feeling of righteousness, or other people will give me their approval.

But what if my only purpose for going to the temple is to seek a refined sense of inspiration for those people that I could go heal, the dead and the living? Not for myself, but for others? My only purpose is to seek to heal and that is all I would go for. I go for no other reason. That is the ship headed in the direction of perpetuity. That takes going to the temple and elevates it to a higher and holier work. It doesn't mean that the work is not holy otherwise. But doing things out of obedience can be elevated even further, if done in a spirit of healing and a nontransactional desire to lift other human beings. If I'm going to receive revelation on how to heal another, then the law of love is invoked.

That reminds me of a story told by Elder Marvin J. Ashton of the Quorum of the Twelve Apostles:

> During an informal fireside held with a group of adult Latter-day Saints, the leader directing the discussion [asked] the question: "How can you tell if someone is converted to Jesus Christ?" For forty-five minutes those in attendance made numerous suggestions in response to this question, and the leader carefully wrote down each answer on a large blackboard. All of the comments were thoughtful and appropriate. But after a time, this great teacher erased everything he had written. Then, acknowledging that all of the comments had been worthwhile and appreciated, he taught a vital principle: "The best and most clear indicator that we are progressing spiritually and coming unto Christ is the way we treat other people." ("The Tongue Can Be a Sharp Sword," *Ensign*, May 1992)

A Catholic monk, Thomas Merton (1915–1968), added to this thought: "Our job is to love others without stopping to inquire whether or not they are worthy. That is not our business and, in fact, it is nobody's business. What we are asked to do is to love, and this love itself will render both ourselves and our neighbors worthy" (letter to Dorothy Day, quoted in Stephen Hand, *Catholic Voices in a World on Fire* [Lulu, 2005], 180). I totally agree. Others' worthiness is not our business—certainly never in heaven or at the Judgment Day, but not on this earth either. That's between them and God. What we're asked to do is love.

Notice the blessings that Merton mentioned happen in both directions: "This love itself will render both ourselves and our neighbors worthy." That's God's boomerang blessings: they return to bless us as well.

THE LAW OF LOVE IN OTHER FAITH TRADITIONS

I often think about Mother Teresa, working in the slums of Calcutta. Every day this Catholic nun from Albania, barely five feet tall, woke up and thought of nothing but to serve the humans around her. She sought nothing back. Every nun makes vows of chastity, poverty, and obedience, but she took a fourth vow—to give "wholehearted free service to the poorest of the poor" (Malcolm Muggeridge, *Mother Teresa Speaks* [San Francisco: Harper Collins, 1971], 113). Mother Teresa managed homes for people who were dying of HIV/AIDS, leprosy, and tuberculosis. She worked with children and the poor in unimaginable conditions in the slums of India. These were people that had absolutely nothing TO give back to her, but she wasn't in it for the transaction. She was in it just out of her pure love of others and of God. In her own words, she was "seeking the face of God in everything, everyone, all the time, and his hand in every happening. Each day I see Jesus Christ in all his distressing disguises" (Mother Teresa, *In the Heart of the World: Thoughts, Stories and Prayers* [Novato, CA: New World Library, 1997]).

Almost every religious tradition that I've been exposed to or that I've studied has elements of the law of love. Latter-day Saints don't own the law of love. There are people all over the world seeking this law of love. It's instinctive, knowing that living without transaction is the higher law. And once you understand it, you see people who are out there teaching it.

David Brooks was invited to speak at a BYU Forum on October 22, 2019. He is a columnist for the *New York Times* and a Jewish man. His speech was titled "Finding the Road to Character," and excerpts appeared in *BYU Magazine* with the title "Seeing Others Deeply" (Winter 2020 issue). In his own words, Brooks named the same thing that Moroni 7 describes. Brooks said, "You can be happy alone. You win a game, you get a promotion, you feel big about yourself. Happiness is the expansion of self. But joy is the merger of self. It is a kind of thing that happens when you forget where you end and something else begins, when you really are seeing deeply into each other."

Brooks talked about a couple that was moving out of a neighborhood that had gone in the wrong direction in their minds. They didn't think it was safe for their kids. And as they prepared to leave it, the woman, Aiesha Butler, looked out and "saw a girl in a pink dress playing in an empty lot with broken bottles. She turned to her husband and said, 'We're not going to leave that. We're not going to just be another family that left.'" In effect, she was saying, "This is a neighborhood we need to heal." And she did. She volunteered and volunteered, and now she runs the community organization. The neighborhood turned around.

Aiesha was looking at people more deeply. She saw—really saw—that girl in the pink dress. And that opened up the conduit for deeper understanding. Aiesha wasn't looking for anything in return from that girl; she just wanted to love her and all the kids like her, to heal the neighborhood. And then, all of a sudden, ways to heal, ways to work together and collaborate, began to emerge, in the spirit of abundance. When Brooks described it, I thought, *That's such an interesting way to think about the law of love.* There are so many dimensions to it. The law of love just keeps unfolding in different ways, from points of view that I had never considered. I came to understand it better.

In that same talk, Brooks described another interesting situation that further illustrates transactional and nontransactional relationships:

> A few years ago there was an Israeli daycare center that had a problem: the parents were coming in late to pick up the kids. So they imposed fines on the parents who came in late. The number of parents who came in late doubled. That is because before, picking up your kid on time was a moral responsibility to the teacher so they could go home. Once the fine was imposed, it was no

longer a moral responsibility; it was an economic trans-action. ("Seeing Others Deeply," *BYU Magazine*, Winter 2020)

This is a brilliant illustration of a relationship that began by being rooted in respect for the teacher's time. Once it became transactional, instead of solving the problem, it became a bigger problem. This shows that when you add the element of transaction, the relationship tends to rot. At the very least, making the relationship transactional didn't solve the problem but actually made it worse.

11

THE LAW OF LOVE
IN RELATIONSHIPS

Transactional love is self-congratulatory and immediately gratifying. I love other people and give them things they want, then I get an immediate reward as they love me in return and give me things I want. But that kind of transactional relationship is shallow and susceptible to decay. It's tempting to treat others as highly paid extras in my life drama. But in truth, each person is an individual child of God with hopes, dreams, fears, and needs—just like me.

Whether it's someone that we just pass on the street; bump into inadvertently in a crowd, even virtually by Zoom; down to the most intimate relationships with a spouse, family member, or dear friend; it doesn't matter—the relationship could be a fraction of a second or a lifetime, but the ask is the same: Can you enter this relationship and extend healing? Can you move beyond all the tendencies for revenge and self-interest?

What is God asking me to do? God is asking me to make a space in this relationship so that I could let the Atonement of Jesus Christ work. What Christ is saying is, "I want to be in the middle of your relationships. I did what I did (meaning accomplish the Atonement) so that I could be in the middle. I want to be there, but I cannot be there unless I'm invited in by some party."

If I'm going to really live my religion in every relationship, I have to invite God in. The Atonement of Christ has to be a part of the relationship so that it can heal.

I don't heal it. Jesus heals it. But I help create a space for it to happen. That doesn't mean that it happens at that moment. Sometimes it doesn't happen at all. People can live in resentment and anger and frustration toward you for your whole life. You try your best to live your religion and sometimes nothing happens. But the space has been created, the opening has been made, and the work is ongoing. You're not working for a specific result. You just want healing and better relationships.

It might be literally just a wave of a hand or a smile or a thumbs-up, or it might be a quick forgiveness for an accidental bump, or a cutoff in traffic, or someone honking at you and it wasn't your fault. Those are just the simple things, let alone the complex things. We do those things with no thought of ourselves, just with the intent to give them some sense of healing, constantly just trying to be a positive force in people's lives. It's just keeping our very first covenant at baptism, our most basic promise: to be "willing to mourn with those that mourn; yea, and comfort those that stand in need of comfort" (Mosiah 18:9).

Confucius said, "The gentleman helps others to realize what is good in them. He does not help them realize what is bad in them.

The small man does just the opposite" (Confucius, *The Analects*, Book XII, 16).

I notice now that whenever I'm in a disagreement, I quickly make an effort to stand in the other person's shoes. I immediately try to see their insecurities, their logic, how they feel wronged, the roots of the conflict. In the end, if healing is the endgame, the only way is to follow Christ's words and example. Stand in their shoes, carry their burdens, essentially lose yourself in the other. Suddenly shards of light begin to shine on solutions. And the solution can be to walk away to protect yourself from harm, to lean in and do something important, or in the end to do nothing but care, listen, and learn.

I have often heard of keeping the focus on oneself instead of pointing fingers at others. This way of dealing with disagreements gives us something we can actually do: look in our own hearts when we bump up against others. Unless we're willing to be really vulnerable around the law of love, we tend to defensiveness. But the truth is that we all need forgiveness. Christ says that He would forgive us, then He turns around and tells Peter to forgive seventy times seven (see Matthew 18:21–22). What is He saying? I need my human brothers and sisters to help me, and I need to help them. And the most important way we can help each other is by making space for healing.

LOOKING FOR RESULTS IN RELATIONSHIPS

As we make space for healing, we may get off course when we treat relationships like measurable, quantifiable experiences. Robert

Daines, Stanford Law professor (and by the way, my stake president), said it this way in a commencement address:

> Institutions [are] bristling with high-powered incentives and monitoring mechanisms primed to issue immediate feedback to help us stay focused on the success of the organization. To get more out of us, the firms and government institutions we work for will offer potent encouragement—partnership, praise, promotion and prestige.
>
> Usually the most important commitments and relationships and people in our lives do NOT have comparable built-in incentive and monitoring mechanisms to tell us how we're doing. You will probably NOT get annual reviews from your loved ones and friends. Your family and close friends will not send you monthly reports on how many hours you have spent with them and whether you are meeting, exceeding or falling below expectations.
>
> Driven, success-oriented people want to make a difference. They want to count for something. This may lead you to focus on projects where you can quickly achieve and measure your success. You may focus on projects and milestones (like billable hours, a brief or bench memo) where you can produce observable results in the short run. This feels good.
>
> But relationships with family and friends, peace of mind, a life of service and faith do not yield immediate results. **Real friendships and raising a family will take**

**thousands of hours of work that produce no imme-
diately visible results.** If you are not careful, a desire
for measurable success will lead you to spend too little
time on these relationships. (Stanford Law commencement address, June 16, 2012, cdn.law.stanford.edu/wp
-content/uploads/2015/08/2012_Speech_Daines.pdf;
emphasis added)

It's absolutely true that there are plenty of things that involve
years of investment with no instant payoff, maybe even no visible
results. For years. The law of love is not a quantitative experience. It
has no merit badge. It has no sense of reward. The roots have to be
losing myself. A complete giving to the other soul.

Ministering can be selfless or transactional. Going to the temple
also. And the difference is intent. Why am I doing it? I ask myself
always, what is my motivation? The power of the law of love comes
as I lose any sense of reward. How can I heal? It's those rare moments
that I have felt a fuller measure of the law of love and the geometric
expansion of spirit. That's the oddity: when I give myself over to another's need completely is when I have received the greatest gifts of
spirit and revelation, FOR MYSELF! The irony is immense.

One of the worst examples of transactional relationships is with
the elderly. Some gradually stop valuing their parents and grandparents because they have "ceased production" and make few tangible
contributions to their lives. When grandparents are no longer useful
to babysit or whatever, they may gradually be valued less. But that
way of thinking undermines the value of each person simply for being who they are, wherever they are, in whatever stage of life.

Older folks often bring wisdom, dependability, and unconditional love. They help shape the future of younger generations with their long view of life. Their stories of surviving the challenges of their own lives can inspire younger family members. And even when they bring none of these things due to declining mental capacity, the elderly have dignity in themselves, simply because they exist as a beloved child of God. A life should never be valued based on its utility. That's not the way God sees us. God loves us for who we are, wherever we are in life.

A nontransactional relationship with the elderly means you love them outrageously, for no reason other than just love, seeking nothing in return. You can still have help in terms of living arrangements that better support your elderly loved one, when that is needed. And you can still set boundaries in terms of time and energy. But whatever you do, you do it out of love, not out of a balance-sheet mentality, like a cost/benefit analysis, assessing a person's usefulness. Love—just love.

And if you just can't get to that nontransactional thinking about the elderly, at least remember that some member of that generation wiped you off when you were a helpless baby, when you weren't much of a contributor either. Besides, one day that elderly person might be YOU. Nobody wants to just become the background music—the elevator music as you go up and down the floors.

THE LAW OF LOVE IN MARRIAGE

I think marriage partners are constantly making on-the-spot judgment calls because of the closeness and constancy of the relationship.

Inevitably the challenge is this: am I in a transactional relationship or not? Every time I think of it as transactional, I land in the wrong place. The best advice I ever got was from Elder Richard G. Scott of the Quorum of the Twelve Apostles. He told me, "Your marriage is a covenant without transaction. It will ask all of you all of the time. If you ever try to make a deal, it will inevitably falter."

Tom Christofferson expanded on this a bit:

> Scorekeeping is fatal: the relationships within a family are not a zero-sum game, and there are no individual winners. Either we all win together, through increased understanding and compassion, or we all lose that growth and accompanying deepened commitment. Every relationship of importance in our lives is enriched when approached with the spirit of greater concern for the needs of the other person. (*That We May Be One: A Gay Mormon's Perspective on Faith and Family* [Salt Lake City: Deseret Book, 2017], 87)

I learned a valuable lesson on the football field that has really helped my marriage. How many times have I thrown an interception? There was a moment when the team looked back at me because it looked like I might have just lost the game.

When I first started in football, I would tell them all the mitigating circumstances—you cut left late, my blockers weren't doing their job—but it inspired no one. At the moment of accountability, I focused on all the mitigating factors instead of taking responsibility. Don't ever do that, especially in your marriage. There are key moments in my relationship when I need to take accountability. If I go with the mitigation route, it is disastrous.

In that moment of truth, when the crowd was booing, when the lights were on and teammates were asking why, I often said, "I screwed it up. My fault. That ball was in my hands. It's now in their hands. But I'll tell you what: let's get a drink of water and let's turn it around and win the game." And the amazing thing was, the moment I took accountability, that allowed the other guys to do the same. Then they would often say, "I cut late" or "I missed the block." But whatever they did or didn't do, it didn't matter. It wasn't a transaction. I accepted responsibility because that's what I needed to do, expecting nothing in return. And paradoxically, my accountability opened up space to heal that rift for all of us, so we could get back in the game.

One of the best things I learned in my football career was to watch for those times in the moment, not later in the locker room or the next day in film. Taking accountability in the moment, right there in front of everyone, before people get too far down the road with their reaction, defuses the situation a lot and brings a healing spirit. Not only is it one of the best things I learned; it's one of the most important things I can teach my kids: the vulnerability to recognize mistakes and the strength to go fix them.

The vulnerability to recognize mistakes applies to even the smallest things. I notice that in some areas, I keep making the same mistakes. Sometimes I forget the same thing at the grocery store fifty times in a row. Okay, that's an exaggeration, but you get my point. Every time, I say, "I screwed up and I'm going to go fix it." Even though I make mistakes more often than I want to admit, my taking accountability right away really helps. As long as a mistake is accounted for, and there is a genuine effort to fix it, there is space for moving beyond the mistake. And on the fifty-first time at the grocery store, I just might get it right.

Back to Reggie White, who tackled me and then asked about my family, transitioning instantly from my opponent to my friend. In a millisecond Reggie could pivot from a ferocious, adrenaline-filled moment to friendly and chatty. I call it having many shoes to wear. Reggie could change to different shoes even in the middle of a game. For me, I finish work, race home, and then I'm the dad to help with homework, or I'm the cook because we need dinner. I find myself going through the rigor of transitioning into different shoes three or four times a day. It helps when I recognize it and tell myself, "I'm wearing different shoes." I need to be focused on what is right in front of me but be able to shift quickly to another pair of shoes in a moment. Life is more spiritually athletic than wearing just one pair of shoes. This idea enables me to be there in those small but important moments, transitioning quickly to being fully present. Because of my love for my wife, I give my marriage 100%, and Barb absolutely does the same.

Here's another point of view from Gary Thomas, an evangelical Baptist minister, from his book *Sacred Marriage*:

> When I asked my wife to marry me, my decision was based almost entirely on what I thought she would bring to the marriage. She looked good; we had fun together; she loved the Lord. And my suspicion is that her thoughts were running in the same direction. Can this guy support me? Do I find him attractive? Would he be a good father?

These aren't bad questions to ask, but once the ceremony is over, if we want to enter a truly Christian marriage, we have to turn 180 degrees and ask ourselves, "How can I serve my mate?" Sacrifice isn't sacrifice unless it costs us something. I've learned to guard not just my servant's actions, but my servant's spirit. If I serve Lisa with little puffs of exasperation, grunting every time I lift a finger on her behalf, I'm exhibiting a proud, false-martyr's spirit, not the attitude of Jesus Christ. (*Sacred Marriage* [Grand Rapids, MI: Zondervan, 2000], 180, 185, 190)

Love is romantic, to be sure. But it is also something else. It's caring for another more than yourself. It's empathy and compassion and sacrifice. It's setting aside your own concerns to lift someone else. For me (I never would have expected this), service IS romantic.

One little service that Barb loves every night is that she loves me to scratch her back with a pen cap. It started early in our marriage when she was pregnant with our first child and was sick in bed for months. It was the only thing that helped her get to sleep. That's how it started. Now that is how we end the night, every night for twenty-two years and counting. It's a part of our romance. She loves it because it puts her to sleep and it's just something she really enjoys. And I could see it as doing service, but it's a tender part of my romance with her. Now I find that even I can hardly fall asleep without doing that for her.

Even just doing mundane household chores is part of my expressing my love for her. Any long-lasting romance has to be rooted in selflessness. Honestly, my relationship with Barb keeps getting better and better. The law of love has protected our marriage in a way that has allowed us to thrive, despite everything that life can throw at us.

THE LAW OF LOVE WITH CHILDREN

It's easier in many ways to apply these nontransactional principles to parenting because most of the time you don't get anything back anyway. When Barb had really hard pregnancies, she was in bed for four or five months and it was brutal. How she did it four times, well, I can't even describe it to you, even though I witnessed it. But I made a commitment at that moment when she was suffering: I'm going to change every diaper, I'll pace back and forth with the baby all night so you can rest, and anything else you can think of. I'm going to do everything I can to be helpful here. Now I look at my kids and they have no appreciation for what either of us did for them. They're not supposed to. They have no concept of it, nor do they remember it. But that's not why we did it, so that they would thank us. We did it out of unfathomable depths of love for these little infants that are growing into their own selves. Parenting is more selfless by nature.

At the same time, parents, especially fathers, can get into this jam where they become controlling, as if parents are the revered source of all goodness, truth, and authority. The mild version of this is telling children to do something "because I said so." But you can really get stuck in there. You can get stuck fast. Some people live there forever and they love it because it offers the feedback loop: I tell kids to do something, they do it, and I get what I want, including that feeling of power when they do what I say.

Man, have I had to live my religion to get some insight into what to do as a parent. It has been complex; it has been challenging. Raising kids is hard—setting boundaries, expecting them to live into their potential without being transactional about it. Sure, the early years are a grace period, so to speak—where children learn obedience through merit-badge theology. It's developmentally age-appropriate. Children learn about cause and effect, they learn that obedience brings rewards, and that they can affect the world around them through their actions. Learning to set goals is good. Stickers and rewards and incentives work, at least at first. But how can we lay that foundation in a way that we can build on it and move beyond it?

A young mother shared with me her journal about her five-year-old son:

> Sunday: Robby got his first tithing receipt!
> Monday: Robby prayed for snow and reminded the
> Lord that he paid tithing.

That's fine—it's age-appropriate for a five-year-old to think that obedience one day earns him answers to prayers the next, and God, please be quick about it already. But too many children get stuck in this concept of looking for rewards from God and from others throughout their lifetimes. They may become disillusioned when prayers aren't always answered the way they want. That "me-me-me" thinking is destructive to real relationships and personal happiness.

Parenting is not how I quarterbacked. In football, it's like, "We need to get across the goal line, and you need to come with me. I'm going to do things that incentivize you to come with me, but we're doing this and we're doing it *now*." At its core was compulsion: "Do not give me any baloney—this is happening." As a parent that was my instinct. A little less adrenaline than in Candlestick Park, but you get the idea.

My children would be more like (metaphorically speaking), "No, I'm heading off the field, I'm going to go get a drink of water, I'm going to sit on the sidelines." And I'm like, "Oh no, oh no, that's not how it's going down." I had this existential moment when I realized that they really are in control of their own lives, which is the way it should be. They might not do it the way I think it should be done. I have found that I need to leave this compulsion behind. No one likes to be forced. Remember, that's Satan's plan: "I will force them to live righteously" (see page 49).

I've taught, I've modeled, I've done everything that I can, and I continue to do those things. I never stop modeling and teaching. Never. But controlling and compulsion are not how it works. I have no weapons and few tools. So it goes back to living my religion: gentle persuasion, meekness, long-suffering, love unfeigned. I swear, every day I think about love unfeigned. Every day. It's not my natural instinct. I'm the can-do guy. But Barb started me on a track of this kind of love for everyone. A lot of people prepared me for it, from my family to my seminary teachers to good friends. But when Barb pulled me onto the track of the law of love, I had nowhere else to go. I needed to find a way forward in the gospel that fit with Barb's instinctive, reflexive love. It started to just come together as I continued to think about it and teach the law of love. And that's why I turn to Barb all the time.

That nontransactional thinking applies to me in the way I parent my children, but it also is a value that I need to teach my children in their own lives. Children too need to learn how to make investments of time that may not have an immediate payout. They need to learn delayed gratification. They need to obey God not out of duty, fear of punishment, or expectation of reward (here or hereafter) but only out of love.

Arun Gandhi spoke at BYU on March 23, 1999. He spoke about how his father Manilal, son of the great Mahatma Gandhi, taught him a big, big lesson, not with fear, but with love:

> When I was 16 years old, we were back in South Africa and living on the Phoenix Ashram that Grandfather had created, which was 18 miles outside the city of Durban in the midst of sugarcane plantations. Our nearest neighbors were two miles away from us. Any time my two sisters and I got an opportunity to go to town and visit friends or see a movie, we would grab the chance and go.
>
> One Saturday my father had to go to town to attend a conference, and he didn't feel like driving, so he asked me if I would drive him into town and bring him back in the evening. I jumped at the opportunity. Since I was going into town, my mom gave me a list of groceries she needed, and on the way into town, my dad told me that there were many small chores that had been pending for a long time, like getting the car serviced and the oil changed.
>
> When I left my father at the conference venue, he said, "At 5 o'clock in the evening, I will wait for you

outside this auditorium. Come here and pick me up, and we'll go home together."

I said, "Fine." I rushed off and I did all my chores as quickly as possible—I bought the groceries, I left the car in the garage with instructions to do whatever was necessary—and I went straight to the nearest movie theater. In those days, being a 16-year-old, I was extremely interested in cowboy movies. John Wayne used to be my favorite actor, and I got so engrossed in a John Wayne double feature that I didn't realize the passage of time. The movie ended at 5:30, and I came out and ran to the garage and rushed to where Dad was waiting for me. It was almost 6 o'clock when I reached there, and he was anxious and pacing up and down wondering what had happened to me. The first question he asked me was, "Why are you late?"

Instead of telling him the truth, I lied to him, and I said, "The car wasn't ready; I had to wait for the car," not realizing that he had already called the garage.

When he caught me in the lie, he said, "There is something wrong in the way I brought you up that didn't give you the confidence to tell me the truth, that made you feel you had to lie to me. I've got to find out where I went wrong with you, and to do that," he said, "I'm going to walk home—18 miles. I'm not coming with you in the car." There was absolutely nothing I could do to make him change his mind.

It was after 6 o'clock in the evening when he started walking. Much of those 18 miles were through sugarcane plantations—dirt roads, no lights, it was late in the night—and I couldn't leave him and go away. For five and a half hours I crawled along in the car behind Father, watching him go through all this pain and agony for a stupid lie. I decided there and then that I was never going to lie again.

I think of that episode often. It's almost fifty years since the event, and every time I talk about it or think about it, I still get goose bumps. Now, that is power. . . . It's a lasting thing. It's a change we bring through love, not a change we bring through fear. **Anything that is brought by fear doesn't last. But anything that is done by love lasts forever.** ("Reflections of Peace," *BYU Magazine*, Spring 2000; emphasis added)

Notice that Arun Gandhi is describing, in his own words, the law of love: fear and coercion doesn't last, but lead to entropy and decay, while nontransactional love lasts forever. It's all of us moving toward that place of centropy and perpetuity, together.

FORGIVENESS, ACCOUNTABILITY, AND ABUSE

When I talk about nontransactional relationships and selflessness, some people say, well, what about people who take advantage of that? What about people who are out to hurt you? That doesn't mean I walk right into that, right? What about abuse? What about relationships that are toxic?[1] What if they have wronged me? Where's the accountability?

These are great questions. Being in a safe AND nontransactional relationship is going to take all the tools in the toolbox.

We live in an entropic world. We have to be smart here. This is not about giving space for abuse or toxicity. Safety is not a transaction. Let me say that again: safety is not a transaction. Basic personal safety (physical, emotional, and spiritual) is the starting point of any healthy relationship, no matter how distant or intimate the connection. But it's not always easy to achieve. In fact, in some relationships, being safe is not always possible. But despite it all, there are still choices that I can make, even in horrific circumstances, regardless of what the other person does or doesn't do. Let's unpack this.

I can start by setting boundaries. Even Jesus didn't try to do it all. Neither did He try to create the world in one day. Even an all-powerful God took six days to get it done.

Remember when Christ was at the pool of Bethesda? Jesus noticed a "great multitude of impotent folk, of blind, halt, withered, waiting for the moving of the water" (John 5:3). He told one man—one man!—to take up his bed and walk, then He "conveyed himself away, a multitude being in that place" (verse 13). All the rest of the multitude were His beloved brothers and sisters too. But for some reason, Jesus was sent to heal that one man, then He left. Like Jesus,

---

1 If you or anyone you know is trapped in an abusive relationship, here's a hotline to reach folks who can help: The National Domestic Violence Hotline: 1-800-799-SAFE (7233), chat live at TheHotline.org, or text START to 88788. It's free and confidential, and someone is available 24/7/365 to help.

we only need to find out what God wants us to do, and do that. "God's will: nothing more, nothing less, nothing else" (adapted from Dr. Frederick Edward Marsh [1858–1931], a minister in the Advent Testimony Movement).

In President Nelson's words, "Are *you* willing to let God prevail in your life? Will you allow His voice to take priority over any other? Are you *willing* to let whatever He needs you to do take precedence over every other ambition?" ("Let God Prevail," *Ensign*, Nov. 2020; emphasis in original).

All of this is to say that even Jesus set boundaries and didn't try to do it all or help everyone. He just did God's will, that's all. Maybe some relationships are not ready for healing right now. Maybe the time is not right, but I can always wake up every morning with a healing intent, with my heart aiming in that direction. In partnership with Christ, I can try to create a space for healing. One day, perhaps my words, my actions, my healing spirit can open the door for Jesus to enter the relationship and heal it.

Next, I can seek the gift of discernment, to recognize a place of danger or toxicity. Some conflicts can be made creative, in a way that is not toxic. I separate the two: creative conflict vs. toxic conflict. With some difficulties or tough personalities, I can find productivity and creative possibilities in the challenge.

I've had coaches like that. Some coaches were tough, but they did bring out the best in me. Even the relationship I had with Joe Montana was challenging and difficult and awkward. But for me it was always productive. I don't know if Joe would say this, but I think the statistics show that both of us were better for it. The tension was creative, not toxic, even when it was hard. Maybe I can turn conflict into creative tension and grow from it, grow with it.

On the other hand, if it's toxic tension, it's abusive and needs to be put aside. We should never be at risk; we should never put up with abuse. I wish that on no one. It's a terrible place to be.

In some relationships, despite my best efforts, sometimes there is not a place to engage right now, and I've got to make myself safe. Even if I have to distance to stay safe, I can do it in a spirit of healing. My capacity is limited by other people's behavior, but it's still my intent to heal, even in abusive relationships. Is there something that I can do that might bring a spirit of healing for me? Something that could start small that could grow? There might be zero that can be done. But it's like a boat that leaves the port in a certain direction. I can point my boat toward healing, with no expectations of return from the other person, no transaction.

Is my boat stuck in the port, stuck in the past, reliving it over and over, looking for revenge? Or is my boat headed in a direction of healing? It doesn't matter how far from port it is. It may take a long time, but that's the direction I'm headed. I can work toward extending forgiveness to others, but from a safe place. And I can take all the time I need.

An anonymous woman shared her experience in an *Ensign* article. She received this advice: "Keep a place in your heart for forgiveness, and when it comes, welcome it in."

She said, "That seemed like weak advice in a way, but the Spirit etched it into my memory, and it became a golden rule to me. On bad days when I was angry, I could at least say to myself, 'I want to forgive, and I will hang on to that as a goal and desire it and welcome it when it comes'" ("My Journey to Forgiving," *Ensign*, Feb. 1997).

Some things need to be said that are not necessarily healing in the moment, but they can be said in a healing way. I think about that same scripture with the four power words: gentle persuasion, long-suffering, meekness, and love unfeigned. Two verses later this phrase shows up: "Reproving betimes with sharpness, when moved upon by the Holy Ghost; and then showing forth afterwards an increase of love toward him whom thou hast reproved, lest he esteem thee to be his enemy" (Doctrine and Covenants 121:43). Sharpness here is clarity, like a camera in sharp focus. I think God is telling me to be honest and to use my reproof (disapproval) not as a weapon but as a tool, and only in the spirit of love. That keeps me from saying something or yelling at a moment when it's not productive. It's tempting to just get it all out, but it makes me feel better for about one second, and then I realize I've created more wounds and less healing. I can try to be honest and still be clear in a calm spirit of love.

Even though I may need to say some things that are not necessarily healing in the moment, I think about healing in the long view—over the next five years, the next fifty years. For some of that time, maybe all of it, I might need to be away from the situation. But no matter what, I want to heal that relationship, even as difficult as that can be. If that's my mindset, I'll end up in the right place. But whether the relationship ever heals or not, my part is to always seek to extend the Atonement of Jesus Christ in any situation.

Revenge belongs to the preparatory law. The law of Moses talked about punishment: "And if any mischief follow, then thou shalt give life for life, Eye for eye, tooth for tooth, hand for hand, foot for foot, Burning for burning, wound for wound, stripe for stripe" (Exodus 21:23–25). Talk about a transactional relationship! But the law of love is a higher, holier law to live into, by getting to a safe place (physically, emotionally, and spiritually), then moving toward healing the relationship through forgiveness while staying safe. The law of love can start in the darkest hole and begin a path back.

Elder David E. Sorensen of the Presidency of the Seventy said it this way:

> I would like to make it clear that forgiveness of sins should not be confused with tolerating evil. In fact, in the Joseph Smith Translation, the Lord said, "Judge righteous judgment" (Joseph Smith Translation, Matthew 7:1). The Savior asks us to forsake and combat evil in all its forms, and although we must forgive a neighbor who injures us, we should still work constructively to prevent that injury from being repeated. A woman who is abused should not seek revenge, but neither should she feel that she cannot take steps to prevent further abuse. A businessperson treated unfairly in a transaction should not hate the person who was dishonest but could take appropriate steps to remedy the wrong. Forgiveness does not require us to accept or tolerate evil. It does not require us to ignore the wrong that we see in the world around us or in our own lives. But as we fight against sin, we must not allow hatred

or anger to control our thoughts or actions. ("Forgiveness Will Change Bitterness to Love," *Ensign*, May 2003)

Elder Jeffrey R. Holland of the Quorum of the Twelve Apostles added:

It is, however, important for some of you living in real anguish to note what [Jesus] did *not* say. He did *not* say, "You are not allowed to feel true pain or real sorrow from the shattering experiences you have had at the hand of another." *Nor* did He say, "In order to forgive fully, you have to reenter a toxic relationship or return to an abusive, destructive circumstance." But notwithstanding even the most terrible offenses that might come to us, we can rise above our pain only when we put our feet onto the path of true healing. That path is the forgiving one walked by Jesus of Nazareth, who calls out to each of us, "Come, follow me." In such an invitation to be His disciple and to try to do as He did, Jesus is asking us to be instruments of His grace—to be "ambassadors for Christ" in "the ministry of reconciliation," as Paul described it (2 Corinthians 5:18–20). The Healer of every wound, He who rights every wrong, asks us to labor with Him in the daunting task of peacemaking in a world that won't find it any other way. ("The Ministry of Reconciliation," *Ensign*, Nov. 2018; emphasis in original)

This is a challenge—a hard challenge. But remember that a Saint is spiritually athletic. We can do hard things.

I don't have to do it all at once, and I may need some time to live into this higher law, but what matters is the direction I'm headed. As always, Christ was our perfect example, when He forgave the Roman soldiers that crucified Him as He hung from the cross: "Father, forgive them; for they know not what they do" (Luke 23:34). He asks us to join Him as we look down from our own agony and move toward forgiveness for those who harm us.

Well, what about accountability? Does forgiveness mean they just get away with it? My response is, well, the accountability was never yours. Even when you're wronged, the wrong sits with the Savior. It's His job, not mine, to judge and to hold others accountable. He sees everything and knows everything—meaning that nobody ever gets away with anything, whether they are held accountable in this life or not. I can "take appropriate steps to remedy the wrong" and "prevent further abuse," as Elder Sorensen said—while still moving in the direction of forgiveness. But the outcome is out of my hands. The rest is up to the Savior.

It's like Jean Valjean in *Les Misérables*, who stole a loaf of bread to feed his family. Sure, it was stealing, but who can say whether it was right or wrong?

In other circumstances, mental health issues may interfere with a person's ability to be responsible for their actions. Only the Savior knows what is in our hearts, not just in our actions. Jesus said, "For I, the Lord, will judge all men according to their works, according to the desire of their hearts" (Doctrine and Covenants 137:9). I can't see into someone else's heart, so I'm in no position to judge. Accountability starts and stops with the Savior.

My goal here is to explain the law of love and nontransactional relationships in a way that doesn't feel threatening, that feels inviting and sweet and ennobling, because that's what it is.

Colleen C. Harrison wrote this parable in her book *He Did Deliver Me from Bondage:*

> One day I dreamed a dream. I was walking up a long, tree-lined lane, and though I was ragged and wounded and still using a crutch to steady myself, I was full of excitement. I had just entered into the last stretch in what had been a long and perilous journey home. Just over the next rise was "the green, green grass of home" and my family waiting to greet me.
>
> Suddenly I noticed another figure hobbling along just ahead of me. Whoever this poor soul was, I could tell that he was in at least as bad a shape as I was. But even with all his wounds, he had made it this far too. My heart went out to him in fellowship, and quickening my pace, I hurried to overtake him, calling out to him, "Brother, wait! Wait for me!"
>
> He stopped and turned. My heart went chill as all my feelings drained from it. I recognized his face. He had been my enemy, the very one who had inflicted the deepest wounds—wounds that had made my journey so slow and painful—wounds that I still bore unhealed. Not him! How could he be here too?
>
> I halted my steps, unable to approach him any further, unwilling to say anything. As he called out "Who's

there? I can't see you," I realized that he was blind. Rather than answer his plaintive cry, I held my breath. Soon he turned, dejected, and shuffled on his way.

I didn't have far to follow him, for just ahead of us was a shining, glorious gate. The boundary that it marked was as definite as if it were guarding night from day. What lay beyond the gate was beyond description, but not recognition. It was Home. Upon my seeing it, childhood memories seemed to flood my mind. Every path and byway was familiar to me. The longing to be there once more became an overwhelming ache within me. It caused me to totally forget my reluctance to approach my enemy, who was even now standing at the gatehouse, speaking to the gatekeeper.

The gatekeeper had his back to me. Still I recognized Him immediately as my Lord and Good Shepherd. He who had carried me throughout much of my journey, ministering to my stubborn wounds. Just as He had promised, He employed no servant here. Suddenly I realized that [my enemy's] eyes were bright and clear, focused upon the face of the Gatekeeper. I realized he was not blind anymore! Then I noted how straight he stood. Eagerly, I threw down my crutch and rushed forward. Maybe I too could be made whole!

Before I could take more than a step or two, I was suddenly aware of the Gatekeeper's words to my lifelong enemy. "There is only one last thing before you are ready to enter in, one last question I must ask."

My enemy! This person who had been responsible for my deepest wounds! He was about to enter in?

The Gatekeeper continued, breaking through my shock. "Are you a friend to every man?"

Taking his gaze from the Gatekeeper's face, the man looked steadily into my eyes, and I knew he was seeing me, *really* seeing me, for the first time. Somewhere inside I trembled. I had known all along that I would have to face the Lord to enter in, but my enemy?

His words pierced my soul. "I am willing to be," he said quietly. Healed and no longer blind, he loved me. Could I, still maimed and crippled as I was, say the same? Could I answer this one last question with an honest yes?

The Gatekeeper seemed to disappear from between us, though I knew He was near. Nothing stood between my enemy and me. He waited for my response with longing meekness in his eyes, unable to enter in without my approbation. And just as surely, I knew I could not enter in without him. My long-harbored resentment and bitterness, or all that lay beyond this last barrier—which would it be? Which would I choose? Why had I waited so long? How had I thought I could avoid this moment?

My first step toward him was still halting, as if crippled, but with each step my strength grew greater and greater. I could feel my wounds healing as I reached for his hands and then his embrace.

[Then] the Gatekeeper and another figure stood with us. With shining countenance the Gatekeeper turned to the other. Speaking my name with that of my former adversary, He said, "Father, these are my friends." As I awoke from the dream, the last impression I had was hearing the voice of the Father, so long awaited, "*Well done. You may all enter in.*"

Speaking of those who would gain only a portion of glory and not a fullness, the Lord said, "Nevertheless, they shall return again to their own place [the one they choose], to enjoy that which they are willing to receive, because they were **not willing to enjoy that which they might have received**" (Doctrine and Covenants 88:32). (Excerpted from Colleen C. Harrison, *He Did Deliver Me from Bondage: Using the Book of Mormon and the Principles of the Gospel of Jesus Christ as They Correlate with the Twelve-Step Program to Overcome Compulsive/ Addictive Behavior and Other Problems*, Revised Edition [Hyrum, UT: Hearthaven Publishing, 2002], 111–14; emphasis in original)

This story got me crying. It's just a dream, but it lays out the work (it won't be easy) and demonstrates the ultimate redeeming power of the law of love. So many situations in life feel irretrievable. Some people say, "I don't even know how to start. Sometimes there is so much anger, and so much dividing us that there is nowhere to go."

But it's about our intent. It might not have words at first, it might not even have real actions at first. Yet like the mustard seed of faith, my intentions are rooted in a desire to heal that other person. Even in the most complex, difficult relationships, I can hold in my heart a constant intent to heal.

Some say, "Asking me to love my enemy? That's too much." Never mind that in Jesus's first major sermon of His ministry, the Sermon on the Mount, He invited us to "Love your enemies, bless them that curse you, do good to them that hate you, and pray for them which despitefully use you, and persecute you" (Matthew 5:44). Some might think, *That's just one of those noble scriptures to study and teach others. You don't actually expect me to live it, do you, Jesus?*

A transactional way of looking at forgiveness sounds like this: "Go ahead, you make the first move." That is, I'll forgive my enemy once they repent and make restitution and ask for my forgiveness; then I will grant them pardon. Sometimes forgiveness works like that. But a nontransactional way of looking at forgiveness sounds like this: "They may never in this lifetime understand how they hurt me. But their sin is between them and God. What this situation asks of me is forgiveness without expecting anything in return, just like God forgives me, unprofitable servant that I am (see Mosiah 2:21). It won't be easy to forgive, and I may not be ready yet, but my boat is heading in that direction, with God's help."

The relationship may never be healed in this lifetime. That part is out of my hands. But if I try to lay the law of love on this situation, if my intent is in the direction of forgiveness and healing, the end result for me is peace—"the peace of God, which passeth all under-standing" (Philippians 4:7). In seeking to heal another, I am healed.

It may sound like most of the stories from my own life that I've shared in this book are the "happily-ever-after" variety. At the same time, I've got plenty of examples where nothing works out temporar-ily but I still feel love and peace. It's trickier to share those stories in detail because of confidentiality, but rest assured that living the law of love is seldom easy or straightforward.

Some people say, I want justice and damnation for my enemy, and I want mercy and salvation for me. But "the world [is] wide enough" for everyone (Lin-Manuel Miranda, "The World Was Wide Enough," *Hamilton* [2015], quoting Lawrence Stern's book *Tristam Shandy*, according to *Hamilton: The Revolution,* by Jeremy McCarter and Lin-Manuel Miranda [New York: Grand Central Publishing, 2016], 272). The law of love shows us the way to broaden our world to include everyone. Everyone. Anything conceived by the law of love is life-creating, life-affirming, and will never die. So why not practice celestial life now? Why not practice Zionistic life, city-of-Enoch style? We can do this, but sure, it's hard.

Ann Madsen had a difficult time forgiving, too. She told this story about meeting with her bishop in a temple recommend inter-view.

I decided to ask his counsel as I tried to forgive someone for long-ago pain and hurt. I had the sense as I brought up the subject that the bishop was reaching up in prayer to know how to teach me. (That was a wonderful moment.) We spoke only a few words, but he seemed to understand exactly how I was troubled.

I explained that even though the person had been dead for several years, I knew I couldn't ignore the problem any longer. He spoke with me of mercy, pity [for the other person]. I said I had tried to feel that and I was still trying. . . . He added, "You say to yourself, 'Someone should have to pay for this. It isn't fair.' But, Ann, Someone has paid for it." I knew immediately that he meant the Savior, and I wondered how I had been so dense for so long, and I began to cry. ("Jesus, the Very Thought of Thee," BYU Women's Conference address, 1997)

As inconceivable as it seems, Christ has already paid for everything that has ever happened to us or ever will happen to us. He asks everything of us, even the nearly impossible task of forgiving our enemy. We cannot shy away from it or else we won't have done what we came here to do, what Jesus is calling us to do: to learn and grow. The law of love is foundational to that supercharged growth. Even if we are not ready to forgive yet, we need to start practicing and understanding the law of love so that we can start to grow into it. Nor should we shy away from its full measure. Because we know, and Christ knows, that on the other side of that tremendously difficult forgiveness is the ultimate healing, the deepest peace. In the end it's the thing that's most good for you, but it's the hardest to do. This journey toward a place of perpetuity requires much more than a half-hearted nod in the general direction of Zion.

Here is another strong, brave woman who had much to overcome:

Julia Nompi Mavimbela (1917–2000), Relief Society president in the Soweto branch, South Africa: In 1981, Julia joined The Church of Jesus Christ of Latter-day Saints (under apartheid in South Africa, just three years after the Church's priesthood/temple ban was lifted worldwide in 1978) and famously kept a picture of the white prophet, Spencer W. Kimball, on her wall despite intense racial tension. This portrait bore a resemblance to the white Prime Minister of South Africa, P. W. Botha, which almost got her house petrol-bombed by freedom fighters were it not for intervention on her behalf from political allies who understood her devotion to both her church and the anti-apartheid cause. She wrote, "Let us dig into the soil of bitterness, throw in a seed, show love, and see what fruits it can give. Love will not come without forgiving others. Where there has been a bloodstain, a beautiful flower must grow." (*Illuminating Ladies II: A Coloring Book of Mormon Women*, illustrated by Molly Cannon Hadfield [Exponent II, 2020], 48)[2]

The law of love is real, vital, and the ennobling piece to the puzzle. Almost every choice we make in relationships is either transactional or not. We can see the results almost immediately at times.

---

2 For more about Julia Mavimbela, see "Latter-day Saints Keep on Trying," by Elder Dale G. Renlund, *Ensign*, May 2015; "Healing the Beloved Country: The Faith of Julia Mavimbela," by Matthew K. Heiss, *Ensign*, July 2017; and the video "Break the Soil of Bitterness" at history.churchofjesuschrist.org/article/break-the-soil-of-bitterness/one-womans-quest-for-healing.

For example, sometimes when I have been in a disagreement, I take a minute to choose the right word, the more healing word. That just changes the conversation and sends a message that I am not in a zero-sum-game fight. I no longer just need to win or compete. Some people go right by it as if to say, *I don't care what you say; I'm getting all I can.* But at other times I've seen that a simple word of gentle persuasion can change the conversation in a second. Most importantly, we need to see that the peace, beauty, and joy that we most want in our lives comes most fruitfully from the law of love.

THE LAW OF LOVE AND OUR LGBTQ+[3] SIBLINGS

My exploration of the law of love really started with our LGBTQ+ siblings. Barb has been an LGBTQ+ ally for decades, starting before we were married. For many years I have listened to people in tears tell Barb how much it meant to them that somebody saw them— *really* saw them and heard them. Her allyship made me think and caused me to really dive deep. My wife power-washed the cultural barnacles off my boat. She takes it right down to steel.

Eventually we were invited to speak at Affirmation in September 2013. Barb was one of the featured speakers, and I spoke as well. Afterward, many young LGBTQ+ individuals and their parents and allies in the audience rushed to the stage to hug her. There was this big group around her. I loved it because I wasn't the center of attention (I'm kind of a natural introvert, believe it or not). Then several young men, after hugging Barb, walked over to me, one by one. Most were post-mission or mid-twenties or so, with essentially the same story.

---

3 Lesbian, gay, bisexual, transgender, and queer or questioning.

They said, "Steve, my dad and I have a broken relationship, and things are hard between us. I would want nothing more than to send my dad a picture with you and me. Because maybe for a minute, since I know how much he loves *you*, he might be able to see this picture and love *me* too, maybe see me in a different light." I remember how desperate these kids were to be accepted by their own parent. Just the pain and the honesty and the integrity of their feelings—wanting to be able to mend their relationship with their dad and heal a little bit—was so raw and real. They didn't want a picture with me for themselves; they wanted a picture with me to heal a relationship, to make some connection with their family. What they were asking was so simple, yet for them so profound. In that simple service, I pulled them close with a teary smile while a friend took the picture. My answer was always "Of course," but what I really wanted to say was, "Can I go home with you? Can we meet with your dad and maybe talk?" Naturally that wasn't practical, but that's the way my boat was headed, that's for sure.

My experience with our LGBTQ+ siblings was the beginning of seeing others in a deeper way. There is always some person whose background is different from mine, that I'm not familiar with, maybe culturally they're a little different from me. I'm always richly blessed when I get to know them. Some of the most spiritual experiences and sweetest blessings of my life have come when I've gotten to know folks that offer me a different life experience than my own. My calling as a "true follower of Jesus Christ" (see Moroni 7:48—all roads lead to Moroni 7) requires me to check my privilege and learn from all that everyone has to teach me. I've learned to "be curious, not judgmental" (attributed to Walt Whitman).

In those moments with my LGBTQ+ siblings, I felt a spirit that I've just never felt in the same way. Certainly, I've had many, many spiritual experiences that are embedded in my soul, but this experience speaking at Affirmation was different. It was enlarging. It was three or four floors up—a heightened experience.

Barb said to me the other day, "Steve, I'm always for the underdog. I'm always for the person that's just not represented or whose voice isn't being heard. I just don't know how else to be." That's what Jesus did when He was on the earth, and what He would do today. Barb instinctively seeks others' healing without transaction. That way of thinking about others doesn't come as naturally to me as it does to her, but at least I can catch the vision of it. This law of love is an amazing truth that I want to share with everyone: that God is right here with us, almost viscerally proximate, and that we're all divine as His children, and that we're here to heal each other.

Those kinds of moments—having everyone gather around Barb because they know she really sees them—happen all the time. Once we were in Orem, Utah, a couple of states away from our home in California, shortly after Prop 8. We stopped to get a frozen yogurt. As we left the shop on the way to the car, we walked past a table of four couples sitting out on the patio. One of the men, a total stranger to us, asked, "Hey, are you Barb Young?"

"Yeah," she replied.

"Well, we want to thank you for all your work to fight discrimination and teach everyone how to love one another."

Barb teared up and said, "That means a lot to me."

I asked, "Where are you from?"

"We're all from the same ward in Alpine, Utah," they responded.

I get teared up just thinking about it even now, mostly for the healing it brought to Barb. It meant so much to Barb and me that total strangers knew and loved her. It was so meaningful that this group of couples out for yogurt, these fellow allies, would tell her how grateful they were to her.

People ask me all the time, "Are you Barb Young's husband?" and I love it. Whether checking in at hotels, or traveling on airplanes, or running into folks in foreign countries, I'm constantly being stopped by folks who want me to be sure to tell her how much they love and appreciate her.

I love being Barb Young's husband, standing in the shadow of her light.

It was LGBTQ+ folks' natural outreach and their spirit of warriorship at the margins that really led me to this whole idea of the law of love. They're being told in some fundamental ways that they're broken, but they understand, "No, I'm not, and I'm trying to figure out how to go forward. And I'm faithful and this gospel resonates with me and I want to stay close. And at the same time there seems to be no place for me in that warriorship."

I have been on football fields watching the toughest players with incredible strength performing phenomenal athletic feats through sheer force of will. I know strong, tough-minded, gritty people. And standing with LGBTQ+ folks, all of a sudden it hit me that that same gritty, tough, warrior kind of human was standing in front of me, but even more, at a different level. I saw them for who they really are. Seeing them that way really brought an incredible, pure love and tremendous respect for their strength. These beautiful people are our warriors—warriors for empathy and understanding. It just propels me forward.

My experience with LGBTQ+ folks is that I always get more than I give. I'm spiritually enlarged by their ability to teach me. It's not like I'm the good Samaritan doing the rescuing here. They are actually teaching me about grit and determination and the law of love and how to live it. Just by my getting involved with them, even a little bit, I gain so much more insight. I am taught. I'm grateful for these warriors in my life.

THE LAW OF LOVE AND INTEGRATION

Every difference is an opportunity.

Right after I joined the 49ers, Bill Walsh called the team together for the first summer practice. He said, "The first thing we are going to do—before we run a play, before we practice—is integrate you as a team."

At that time, in 1987, we immediately thought of race. We had Black guys and white guys and Polynesian guys, and we thought he wanted to integrate us racially. The football locker room can be a really great, cool space for a sense of brotherhood amongst races.

But Bill said, "I'm not talking just about race. I'm talking about every other thing that separates you from another person, whether it's what school you went to, what position you play, what religion you are, what politics you support, what language you speak, or what socioeconomic background you're from: whatever it is that separates you. In the locker room and the bus and the plane and the lunchroom, I do not want you sitting with the people that you're just culturally more familiar with."

All the quarterbacks would sit together because we knew each other. And I didn't really know the other guys. I didn't know the defensive backs or especially the new guys. Bill would come into the locker room or the cafeteria and say, "Get out." You had to pick up your tray and go sit with someone you didn't know. Bill said, "I'm going to force you to get to know each other." His goal was to have everyone on the team know something an inch or two deep about each other. That way, he said, "when you are in tough circumstances, you'll get into the huddle and look at each other and your integration at that moment will connect you instead of acting like a bunch of independent contractors. You will actually know each other and will fight for each other."

And he forced it. It was uncomfortable and we hated it, but he was absolutely right to do it.

I never put this together before, but he was asking us to do what David Brooks told us: see each other deeply. Bill was thinking, *I know that if I can get you guys integrated and understanding each other better, then when it's third and seven in Lambeau Field in the snow, and it's freezing cold and you're down by four and there are two minutes left and we've got to go the length of the field—the more integrated you are, the better chance we have to win.* So the way to victory for football he described as integration, but he was essentially saying, if we can learn to see each other more deeply, we can win. Not because of what play we call, but because of how connected we are. That's how he taught it.

The same is true of any group in life. Staying separate and acting like a bunch of independent contractors limits our possibilities. But when we know each other better and start to act like a team—from a small work group to a team as large as the human family—we can accomplish astonishing things together.

Race, religion, language, pay grades, the jobs you're asked to do, unique talents—there is no more different group of human beings than the fifty people in an NFL locker room. How do you get everyone moving together in the same direction toward the same goal? There is an underpinning of accountability and a sense that I do care about your success, even more than my own. Conflicts and problems still do come up, but with that foundation of accountability, most of the time you can find your way through them. Without that accountability and genuine caring about the other person, teams just go into the sink. They rot. Fast.

You can often see this kind of separation visibly in the Church. A friend in the stake presidency says that he sits on the stand and looks over the congregation and sees groups of people sitting together who look like each other. We can do better at picking up our mental "cafeteria tray" in church and going over and sitting with someone different from us in some way, learning from them and seeing the world a little differently. It takes effort, but it's worth it. It makes us all better as we become more what Jesus wants us to be: one close-knit human family.

Today we're seeing this incredible conversation that's needed to be had around race. The only way to have it is in a vulnerable, non-transactional space. Long-suffering, gentle persuasion, meekness, and love unfeigned can power us through the barriers that keep us apart, so that we can all enjoy the full measure of what makes each person unique and amazing.

12

BRINGING IT TOGETHER

E very lesson I teach somehow ends up here, at the law of love. Those moments of transfigured eyesight, those shards of light—it all came together for a woman in the back of my Gospel Doctrine class named Nancy Haight.

Nancy raised her hand and said, "Steve, I think I felt this. I think I've felt this exact thing. I was in a conflict and we went back and forth as I was trying to show how wrong this other person was. And suddenly I was given this ability to see. In my mind I saw her in this most glorious, beautiful place. All of a sudden it wasn't about the conflict. It was as if I saw her from end to end. It's hard to explain in words, but it was like I saw her from the beginning. Nothing mattered in that moment other than the love I felt for her, and who she was, how vital she was and how alive. It just overwhelmed me, that love for her, and it brought me to tears. Then the feeling went away, like I wasn't able to hold it, but I had it."

When she finished, I thought to myself, *That's it, right there. That's the law of love*. She added, "I have sought that feeling ever since. That feeling I had for her, the love that happened in that moment and how I saw her is how I want to always feel. And ever since then, I've longed for that feeling. I want it to be more a part of my life."

Nancy's experience is exactly how we start to prepare for a perpetual, celestial, Zion society. We're not prepared to live in this space, yet. But when we take the challenge of Moroni 7, to "pray unto the Father with all the energy of heart, that ye may be filled with this love" (v. 48), I think that we can start to prepare to be in that perpetual space, together.

Experiencing literal transfigured eyesight allows us to see people deeply. Not just more deeply in what they're doing and who they are today, but to see them more deeply through time and space. It's indescribably ennobling and fulfilling.

THE CAR ACCIDENT[1]

I was the recipient of the law of love in the most impossible situation you can imagine. It happened when I was a junior at BYU, heading home to Connecticut for the summer. I got a call from my former bishop's wife, Bonne Simmons from Scarsdale, New York. Her nineteen-year-old daughter Jill was a freshman at BYU. Jill was like a little sister to me. She was a great athlete, and we had been close friends ever since I had dated her older sister Tori during high school.

---

1 A version of this story appeared in *QB: My Life Behind the Spiral*, by Steve Young with Jeff Benedict (Boston/New York: Mariner Books/Houghton Mifflin Harcourt, 2016], 73–76.

Bonne told me that Jill was planning to drive home from Provo. Concerned about Jill making the cross-country journey alone, Bonne asked if I would be willing to accompany her daughter. I really wanted to fly, but the Simmonses were practically family, so I agreed.

Jill and I left Utah on a Friday night around 10:00 p.m. A third friend, a BYU student from Idaho, decided to ride along at the last minute. He hopped in the back. Jill took the passenger seat. I drove.

I took I-80 and drove through the night while the two of them slept. At around 7:00 a.m. we stopped for breakfast at McDonald's in North Platte, Nebraska. Even after breakfast, I was beat, so Jill said she would drive for a while. I moved into the front passenger seat and fell asleep immediately.

About thirty minutes later I awoke to the sensation of bumping. Jill was slumped over, her head against the driver's side window, and the car was speeding across the wide highway median. I grabbed the wheel, but the front of the car dug into the wet ground and the car flipped over and over. I was not wearing a seat belt, and I bounced from side to side as the car rolled four times. There were no airbags in those days. Even so, I felt like something was shielding me.

The car finally came to a stop on its wheels. The student in the back was badly hurt but conscious. Jill wasn't moving, and she was hanging out the driver's side window. I had no injuries. Not even a scratch, except when I cut my wrist climbing through the broken window. Then I pulled Jill out and laid her on the grass. She wasn't breathing.

I gave her mouth-to-mouth. "C'mon, Jill. You gotta breathe," I said in between breaths. "C'mon, Jill. Don't leave me. Stay with me, Jill."

Few cars were on the highway that morning. But some stopped and people got out to help. "What's happening?" one guy yelled.

"Call an ambulance!" I shouted. I tried frantically to revive Jill. "Please, Heavenly Father, let her live."

It seemed like she was starting to breathe, but she remained unconscious. I cleared her long, dark hair away from her eyes. "Jill, you can't go!" I yelled. "Come back." I wanted so badly to hold her, but I had to keep performing mouth-to-mouth. I feared she would die if I stopped. My tears flowed.

It took almost thirty minutes for the ambulance to arrive. It felt like forever. While I was waiting for the ambulance, it dawned on me that I was an ordained elder. Desperate, I placed my hands on Jill's head and administered a priesthood blessing. I believe fiercely in miracles and angels, and I called for every available one to bring her back right at that moment.

Finally the ambulance arrived. The paramedics placed her on a stretcher and loaded her into the ambulance. I hopped in a police cruiser and followed the ambulance to the emergency room.

When we reached Good Samaritan Hospital in Kearney, an officer pulled me aside. "She didn't make it," he said solemnly. Jill was gone.

I went into shock. "What do you mean she didn't make it? She can't be gone! She can't be!" I just couldn't believe it. This was the first time I had experienced the sudden death of a loved one, and it completely overwhelmed me. I felt so alone. And so responsible.

How am I going to face her parents? They trusted me to get Jill home, and I didn't make it. That awful feeling of responsibility tormented me. *I was there! I was sitting right next to her!*

The next day I caught a flight out of Omaha. I cried the whole way home. I told myself I should not be alive. I had been in the front seat too. I hadn't even been wearing a seat belt. I had thousands of emotions. Most of them were guilt. I was supposed to be driving Jill home; instead I was flying home without her. It was the heaviest feeling I had ever experienced in my life.

I never wanted to be closer to God than at that moment. *Please, Heavenly Father, help me get through this. What do I say to her parents?* These thoughts went through my head the whole way home.

My mom and dad were waiting when I landed at LaGuardia Airport. There was nothing they could say to console me. We drove directly to Scarsdale, and the moment Ted and Bonne saw me they wept. So did my parents. So did I. The reality of the tragedy hit all of us at once.

The family suspected that Jill had fallen asleep at the wheel. They also wondered if she'd had a seizure. But no explanation could make things any easier.

When Bonne and Ted saw me, you could see that they were so worried—*about me*. The first time I walked in and hugged them, they said, "We've been so concerned about you. Are you okay?" That's the spirit that they brought to that moment. They had been broken in a way that only parents can break, and still they were thinking about me.

In all the crushing guilt I felt, Bonne pulled me aside. She looked me in the eye and said, "Steve, this is not your fault. Do not ever think about this with guilt. There is no guilt in falling asleep after driving all night. I want you to never forget that I am so grateful that you were there. It means the world to me that you were there, so Jill wasn't alone in her last moments. She had you there with her. Thank you for being there."

Remember how the law of love works, that it's the way your boat leaves the harbor? In the most tragic circumstances for a parent, Bonne responded in a completely empathetic way. She tried to stand in my shoes. Of all the times that she had every right to stand in her own shoes, in all the grief, that moment was it. And if she had, that would have been fine and completely understandable. But Bonne did something else, something almost incomprehensible. In that moment, immediately, without reservation, she exuded the full measure of the law of love and put me on a path of healing.

There was nothing transactional about it. Bonne was not seeking anything but my healing. She brought transfigured eyesight to that moment and changed everything about the experience. Suddenly it was good that I had been there with Jill—not terrible that I was there, or my fault that I was there. That was a shift in perspective that only the law of love could bring. It took quite a while for it to really sink in until I believed it.

And in the spirit of a wounded healer, that perspective was healing for Bonne too, creating a virtuous cycle. She told me, "I can talk to you, and you can make me feel better like no one else can because you were there. I trusted you and you did not break my trust."

Honestly, it didn't make it easier, or less tragic or difficult, but it created a space for the Atonement of Jesus Christ to work. If I had been at fault, I still would have had to deal with it. The law of love doesn't change accountability or obedience or anything. It just creates a space that allows Christ's Atonement to be a part of our mortal existence.

In every interaction, every relationship, if I'm focused on the law of love, it brings solutions that I never would have considered. I always say that the law of love is undefeated. It just keeps healing.[2]

---

2   More about this story from *QB: My Life Behind the Spiral*, 138: "Prior to the accident I had thought often about God's power to heal, but it wasn't until after the crash that I learned what that really means. As time went on, I started to accept that I had done all I could. I also got a peaceful reassurance in my mind that Jill was doing very well in heaven. It was a spiritual confirmation that she was okay.

"At that point, I asked myself: *How are you going to live the rest of your life?* I thought about that car repeatedly flipping over, and how I felt like I was floating in a pocket of air. And how, miraculously, I was unscathed.

"I took it this way, as a message—*You've been spared and you'd better figure out why.* I felt obligated to live my life in a way that would never dishonor that experience.

"From that day forward I would hear Jill's voice whenever I was doing something—or about to do something—I might regret. I don't mean I would literally hear her voice. But in my mind I could picture her saying, *Steve, what are you doing?* And I would say to myself: *You're right. I need to fix this.* This helped me make last-minute adjustments at critical junctures of my life when I was about to do something that felt wrong.

"I don't want to come across as some moralist or someone who doesn't make mistakes. I'm neither. The point is that I floated in air for a reason. For me, walking away from that accident became a defining moment. The experience committed me to living my life in a more meaningful, Christlike way.

"Jill became my guardian angel."

Epilogue

At last it's on paper. I've talked about the law of love in so many situations, in so many contexts, for so many years. I've wrestled with it and tried to figure it out and tried to live the law of love: loving as God loves, seeking another's healing, expecting nothing in return.

I'm the practical guy. I'm the one trying it and seeing if it actually works. The law of love is not just a theory; it has to work.

If it's true on the football field, if it's true in business, if it's true in church, if it's true in my family and my relationships, if it's true on the street, it's the truth. And I'm here to tell you, it's the truth. I still have plenty of challenges, but after coming to understand the law of love, there are fewer and fewer places where I get stuck for very long.

Many people listen to the law of love and say, "Oh yeah, I'm going to go try that. Nice idea." The worst thing you could do is read this book and put it away and say, "Thumbs up, Steve, good job." The law of love is not just some nice idea. It is THE way to your deepest desires, the most righteous yearnings of your heart—that place of perpetuity where nothing rots or decays, that Zion, that place of celestial peace where Christ the Healer has alchemized all pain into beauty. The only way to receive those things you most want is through the law of love.

Don't stop here. Up next is trying to distill everything you read up to now into three pages that you can stick on your refrigerator or mirror. Don't just shut this book and put it on the bookcase. Take a step—in any order, doesn't matter—whatever is speaking to you—and try it. Taste it. Not to put something else on your already-too-long list of things to do. Not to clutter up your life with another nice goal, but to shift your mindset to this expansive worldview that will help you with everything on your to-do list. As you seek to shift to a law of love mindset, seeking another's healing with no expectation of anything in return, you may be surprised to see that healing comes to you as well, and you discover that the thing you want most is finally in reach: that place of perpetuity and love.

So this is my personal path forward. With the law of love as my guiding light, my steely foundation of faith, I can stare into the enormity of human foibles. From polygamy, racism, difficult issues in Church history, sexism, queerphobia,[1] to anything else that can destabilize my relationship to the institutional Church, I can stare

---

1 Many use the word *homophobia* instead of *queerphobia*. But *homophobia* is usually applied only to LGB individuals (lesbians, gays, and bisexuals), overlooking TIA+ (transgender, intersex, asexual, and many other identities, such as nonbinary and pansexual). Blaire Ostler explains her positive use of the inclusive umbrella term *queer* in her book *Queer Mormon Theology: An Introduction* (By Common Consent Press, 2021), 8–10.

at it, chew on it, and own it. I can find the grace to manage through it without flinching. It can be devastatingly heavy and painful, but I can go back to the fundamental message of the Restoration, which is this: every single person on earth has a divine heritage from loving Heavenly Parents who knew us before; They have a plan for our growth on this earth; and Christ came to heal us and save us. All those pieces were present in various religions in different ways before Joseph Smith's time, but the Lord brought them all together through Joseph in the Restoration. Every aspect of Christ's message should propel us outward to bring healing and to extend the atoning power of Christ to everyone. Every soul is rooted in faith from their very first step into mortality, and we are called to provide more space for that trajectory of faith. It's the call for each of us to rise up to Christ's message of inclusion and love.

I heard something powerful that informs this thought. This is from a message about the Constitution (of all things) from John Durham Peters, a professor at Yale:

> We officially believe the [U.S.] Constitution to be an inspired document.[2] And yet, the Constitution was a profoundly flawed document. It endorsed slavery; it actually awarded money via taxation and representation to slave states; it excluded women from voting. Race and gender [discrimination]: two of the great sins that our nation has been involved in. And yet, how do we recognize it to have been inspired?

---

2 For example, see Dallin H. Oaks, "Defending Our Divinely Inspired Constitution," *Liahona*, May 2021.

Inspiration does not preclude imperfection, which may not even be a strong enough word, [more] like grotesque abuse—there is no other word for slavery. How could that be inspired?

To me, that is a really rich way of applying an atonement theology to the crimes of history. This is very fruitful in terms of thinking about the Church's very complicated racial, racist past. The Atonement [of Jesus Christ] can substantively change the past and bind the future. We think of the future as open-ended and the past as fixed. The Atonement flips that. That's one of the many marvels of it. (*Faith Matters*, episode 87, 33:31)

That idea—simultaneously inspired and flawed—is enormously freeing and energizing, when I thought I had been painted into a corner with no way out. Documents like the Constitution and organizations and people (including myself) can be simultaneously inspired and flawed. I don't have to just slog my way through it and try to avoid the catastrophes; I can actually thrive as I move toward a vision of the future that is exponentially better and grander than we can possibly imagine.

To think that Christ's Atonement can literally change and heal past crimes of history? That Christ could alchemize even all those ashes? That takes all the flames and fires everywhere and gives me a way to not only own them but even use them to burn off the fog between me and the supreme radiant light of God. When I have to clear away everything else, I take it right down to the core. And what's at the core? It's the law of love.

The law of love is Christ's finishing and final message. It is supreme and cannot be muddied. It draws all other laws to it, as an invitation. It's the only law that can live perpetually and fully and create forever places in the universe—forever places like Zion, heaven, the celestial kingdom—these places of perpetuity. Without the law of love, all other laws eventually fail. With it, all laws flourish and can find their full measure. It is the fulfillment of the promises: deep and abiding peace, power, progeny, and purpose.

May the law of love guide us all and take its place in each of our hearts as supreme and perpetually connected to heaven. Christ's hands are always open, palms up, to receive us, always and forever.

How would you like to sum up the whole entire gospel, all in one word? If you've read this far (and thanks for sticking with me here), you can probably guess what that one word might be. The Apostle Paul said it: **"For all the law is fulfilled in one word**, even in this; Thou shalt **love** thy neighbour as thyself" (Galatians 5:14).

One more time: the law of love is undefeated. It works on the football field, in business, in church, in every relationship. The law of love can provide a path forward when everything else has been exhausted. It can work in your life too.

How to Move Forward

IMPLEMENTING THE LAW OF LOVE
IN ALL SPHERES OF MY LIFE

The law of love: loving as God loves, seeking another's healing, expecting nothing in return.

What should be my first steps to accomplish this change in perception, this shift in mindset? It seems a little counterintuitive to talk about steps, since the law of love calls us to BE more than to DO. It calls us to think in new ways. At the same time, there are things that we can actively do to try to move toward nontransactional, healing relationships in every aspect of our lives.

> ### Consider my relationship with God.
>
> Do I see God as an ATM or a celestial Santa Claus? I just try to be really good, ask for what I want, and God brings me stuff? I can consciously work to connect with my *Heavenly Parents* and work toward obedience to the commandments out of nothing more than my love for Them. Jesus said simply, "If ye love me, keep my commandments" (John 14:15). Ironically, this is the way to receive those very blessings I desire—not by seeking them, but by seeking nothing more than God's glory, and then those blessings come. "For whosoever will save his life shall lose it: and whosoever will lose his life for my sake shall find it" (Matthew 16:25). The best way to do this—to find one's life—is to seek others' healing (see next step).

> ### Consider my relationship with others: in my family, in my workplace, in my neighborhood, in my congregation. Do I seek nothing more than their healing, expecting nothing for myself?
>
> I can notice each time I feel disappointed that I didn't get what I wanted from the relationship. I can examine my heart to see if I'm looking for a transaction in return for my efforts toward others. I can remind myself that all people are on their own journeys, not just highly paid extras in my life who are placed on this earth for my convenience. My job is to forget myself and see how I can lovingly support them in their journeys. How can I help them to find out how good they can get? Remember we are co-sojourners in faith with every human. How can I see others not just as they are today, as a collection of good or bad decisions, but to see them as eternal beings? How can I bring aid to every relationship that I have? It's in the intent. My North Star is exactly that: healing others is my only intent. We must love as God loves.

In the Church, I can make sure all my actions are motivated by nothing but love for the other person. I aim for principle-based Church service, not transactional.

Ministering? The goal is love, nothing else—not a check in the box, not the *appearance* of caring for the family or the person. Missionary work? The goal is loving the other person on their own journey, not baptism or reactivation. Sure, it would be nice if those things happened, but that's not the goal. Church service? Not going through the motions but showing forth love unfeigned. Everyone is on their own journey with God, not the journey I think they should be on. Their journey is between them and God—it's none of my business. I'm just here to seek to heal and to love them. That kind of love is a gravitational pull toward covenant-keeping. The Church is a hospital. Sometimes you're the doctor and sometimes you're the patient, but healing is the desired outcome. Words such as *judgment, elite, elect*, and *special* are most often found on the preparatory track, not the finishing track, and all of them tend to rot over time.

I ask myself always, what is my motivation? What is my intent?

The power of the law of love comes as we lose any sense of reward. How can I heal others? In rare moments I have felt the full measure of the law of love and the geometric expansion of that spirit that I feel. That's the irony: I receive the greatest gifts of spirit and revelation FOR MYSELF as I give myself over to another's need completely.

If I find this hard to do, Moroni promises that we can "pray unto the Father with all the energy of heart, that ye may be filled with this love, which he hath bestowed upon all who are true followers of his Son, Jesus Christ" (Moroni 7:48).

That suggests that this unconditional, pure love of Christ is a *gift* that can be *bestowed* by God to anyone. In other words, my role is to pray with all the energy of my heart that I may be filled with this love, and God will bestow this love upon me, says Moroni 7.

I can repeat the four power words to myself like a mantra:

gentle persuasion, long-suffering (patience), meekness (meaning that I seek that higher power in how I behave and how I think), and love unfeigned (genuine, sincere, nontransactional love). When I hit a bump in the road, I seek to overlay those four power words, those four qualities, on the situation. How can I show more gentle persuasion, more long-suffering, more meekness (humility before God and others), more love unfeigned?

In the end we must be rooted in fundamentals:

We are divine in nature. God loves and cares about us intimately and specifically. We were together before this life. Each of us chose to take a body in faith. We are here for an education to be more like God. Christ can heal and redeem everyone. We can help Him. To do it we must LOVE like GOD!

Feedback Welcome

What in this book resonated with you? Do you have any stories of how the law of love has worked in your life? Email lawoflove@foreveryoung.org

Acknowledgments

This book is the fruit of my abundant marriage with Barb and the fruit of my many, many wonderful relationships with both family and friends all over the world that I have had the blessing of rubbing shoulders with.

It wouldn't have been written without the constant urging of my brother and sister-in-law Tom and Stacy Young, my great friend Richard Ostler, and Shauna Doughman, who sat through fifteen years of my Gospel Doctrine classes and wouldn't let me off the hook until I got it written down.

Once I got it out of my head and onto paper, there was no one more vital to this project than the best editor in the world, Marci McPhee. Marci was a trusted source of inspiration, and without her, this couldn't have been done half as well.

Editor's Note

ABOUT STEVE YOUNG

Steve Young is the stuff of which living legends are made. His journey is not typical, nor is it over.

His roots are in Salt Lake City, where he was born, and Greenwich, Connecticut, where he grew up. He was a straight-A student with a photographic memory who graduated from Greenwich High School as an All-State athlete in football, basketball, and baseball.

At BYU he won All-American honors in football and was pegged as the number-one draft choice of the NFL before choosing to join the Los Angeles Express of the USFL. He went on to play for the San Francisco 49ers for thirteen seasons and was a two-time NFL MVP, a Super Bowl MVP, and a first-ballot Hall of Fame inductee in a stellar career over eighteen seasons.

While playing in the NFL, Steve earned a law degree from BYU. After retiring from the NFL, Steve began a second career in private equity, cofounding HGGC in 2007.

EDITOR'S NOTE

Along with his wife Barb, Steve is the founding chair of the Forever Young Foundation, a global charity whose mission is passing on hope and resources for the development, strength, and education of children in Northern California, Arizona, Utah, and Ghana, Africa. Forever Young Foundation is consistently a top-rated charity on Charity Navigator. Steve and Barb have both been involved in many other philanthropic efforts, including their many years of work on behalf of their LGBTQ+ friends, family, and community.

This book is your chance to hear the principles that guide Steve's life, in his own words.

For me, this book contains answers to a prayer that I had been praying for three years. Steve's fresh ideas about solid gospel principles pointed me toward a way out of my own stuck place.

Whether you came to this book for the football stories or to better understand the Christlike principles that guide the man behind the legend, there is something for you in these pages. And it just might change your life for the better, too.

—Marci McPhee, editor
marcimcpheewriter.com

STEVE YOUNG is a two-time NFL MVP, a Super Bowl MVP, and a first-ballot Hall of Famer. A key member of ESPN's weekly coverage, Young holds undergraduate and law degrees from Brigham Young University. He lives with his family in the San Francisco Bay area. He is president and co-founder of HGGC, a private equity firm, and founder of the Forever Young Foundation, a global charity for children, which he co-chairs with his wife, Barb.